CUBE
BOOK

WONDERS OF AMERICA

WHITE STAR PUBLISHERS

text
ELIZABETH HEATH

graphic design
CLARA ZANOTTI

graphic layout
MARIA CUCCHI

editorial coordination
LAURA ACCOMAZZO
VALENTINA GIAMMARINARO

© 2010 EDIZIONI WHITE STAR S.R.L.
VIA CANDIDO SASSONE, 24
13100 VERCELLI - ITALY
WWW.WHITESTAR.IT

○ The Statue of Liberty was installed in 1886.

ISBN 978-88-544-0586-8

1 2 3 4 5 6   15 14 13 12 11

Printed in China

CONTENTS
WONDERS OF AMERICA

1 • The Golden Gate Bridge rises out of the fog of San Francisco Bay, California.

2-3 • Half Dome, easily the most recognizable feature in Yosemite National Park in eastern California, towers over the Tuolumne Meadows wilderness.

4-5 • Central Park cuts a verdant swath through Manhattan Island. Real estate overlooking the park is some of the most expensive in New York City.

6-7 • Strict zoning laws have kept California's Big Sur, seen here along Pacific Coast Highway 1, a sparsely populated area of wild and pristine beauty.

8-9 • The continuously spraying Fly Geyser sits on a bed of deposited minerals in the Black Rock Desert of Nevada.

10-11 • Denali National Park is the home of Mount McKinley (Denali in native Athabaskan language), at 20,320 feet (6,194 m) the tallest mountain in the United States.

15 • George Washington and Thomas Jefferson are two of four U.S. Presidents whose likenesses are carved into South Dakota's Mount Rushmore National Memorial.

Introduction

A FIRST-TIME VISITOR TO THE UNITED STATES OF AMERICA MAY RIGHTLY ASK, "WHERE TO BEGIN?" HOW DOES ONE ATTEMPT TO DISCOVER A COUNTRY SO VAST AND VARIED, AND ONE THAT OFFERS SO MANY WORTHWHILE AND DIVERSE EXPERIENCES? START IN ITS GREAT CITIES? BUT WHICH ONES? NEW YORK OR WASHINGTON? MIAMI OR CHICAGO? SAN FRANCISCO OR LOS ANGELES? OR DO WE FIND AMERICA IN THE COUNTRYSIDE – IN ITS PRIMEVAL FORESTS, ON A HIKING TRAIL IN ONE OF ITS NATIONAL PARKS, IN THE SANDS OF ONE OF ITS OCEAN BEACHES OR ON THE SIDEWALK OF ONE OF ITS SMALL TOWNS?

AMERICA CONFRONTS BOTH VISITORS AND RESIDENTS WITH THESE DIFFICULT CHOICES OF WHAT TO SEE AND WHERE

16-17 ● Colorful Victorian houses, with characteristic "gingerbread" trim, glow in the evening light, with San Francisco's Financial District lit up in the background.

Introduction

TO GO. FOR EVERY BLOCK OF A CITY STREET REVEALS A RICH MOSAIC OF SIGHTS, SOUNDS AND SMELLS, FROM TOWERING SKYSCRAPERS TO QUAINT VICTORIAN NEIGHBORHOODS, FROM HONKING HORNS TO A PLETHORA OF SPOKEN LANGUAGES, FROM A HIDDEN ROSE GARDEN TO THE AROMA OF COUNTLESS VARIETIES OF ETHNIC CUISINE. EVERY WALK IN THE FOREST OFFERS A NEW BIRDSONG, A FRAGILE WILDFLOWER, AND A PRECIOUS MOMENT OF SOLITARY COMMUNION WITH NATURE. EVERY DRIVE ALONG A COASTAL ROAD OR HIGHWAY DISCLOSES A SECLUDED BEACH, A BUSTLING BOARDWALK OR A HISTORIC LIGHTHOUSE. THE WALLS OF EVERY CANYON CHANGE COLOR WITH THE SHIFTING LIGHT, NO TWO WAVES CRASH THE SAME WAY AGAINST A ROCKY BEACH, AND EVERY MAIN STREET IN EVERY SMALL TOWN

Introduction

POSSESSES IT OWN UNIQUE CHARM AND CHARACTER.

MUCH OF THIS VOLUME IS DEVOTED TO HUMAN INTERAC-TION WITH THE LAND THAT COMPRISES THE UNITED STATES. FROM A RUSTIC RED BARN SET AGAINST ORDERLY, ROLLING FIELDS OF CORNSTALKS TO THE DAZZLING UNREALITY OF LAS VEGAS OR THE ARCHITECTURAL WONDER THAT IS THE GOLD-EN GATE BRIDGE, THESE PHOTOGRAPHS SHOW US HOW AMERICANS HAVE WORKED FOR AND AGAINST NATURE AND, MORE RECENTLY, ON HER BEHALF. THEY ARE A TESTAMENT TO THE INDOMITABLE AMERICAN SPIRIT – THAT DESIRE TO IN-NOVATE, IMPROVE AND PROSPER, LIVE A BETTER LIFE THAN OUR ANCESTORS DID AND LEAVE A BETTER WORLD FOR FU-TURE GENERATIONS.

STILL MORE PHOTOS SHOW US AN AMERICA WHICH HAS

Introduction

EXISTED FOR MILLIONS OF YEARS, LONG BEFORE THE EARLI-
EST HUMAN ACTIVITY AND LONGER STILL BEFORE THE AR-
RIVAL OF EUROPEANS. THE ROCKY MOUNTAINS, THE GRAND
CANYON, THE VOLCANOES OF HAWAII AND THE GLACIERS OF
ALASKA HAVE GROWN, SHRUNK, ERUPTED AND SHIFTED FOR
EONS UPON EONS, AND SILENTLY REMIND US OF OUR SHORT
TIME HERE ON EARTH. IN THESE IMAGES, PERHAPS MORE
THAN ANY OTHERS, WE CAN APPRECIATE THE SHEER VAST-
NESS AND VARIETY OF THE UNITED STATES.

AND SO AMERICA, FOR HER RANGE OF ENVIRONMENTS
AND SETTINGS, FROM CITY TO COUNTRYSIDE AND FROM
CANYON TO COAST, FOR ALL HER REGIONAL LOYALTIES, PO-
LITICAL DIFFERENCES, PHILOSOPHICAL IDENTITIES AND HER
BROAD MIX OF COLORS, LANGUAGES AND CREEDS, REALLY IS

Introduction

ONE PLACE. FOR THESE DIFFERENCES, BE THEY GEOGRAPHIC OR CULTURAL, ARE WHAT WEAVE THE VERY FABRIC OF THE NATION. THEY ARE WHAT FORM THE AMERICAN IDENTITY, HARD TO DEFINE AS IT MAY BE, AND WHAT TIE ALL THESE VASTLY DIFFERING PARTS TOGETHER TO FORM THE UNITED STATES, IN ALL ITS BEAUTY, GRANDEUR AND NUANCE.

18-19 • The rich soil of eastern Washington's 3,000-square-mile (7,770 skm) Palouse region makes it a prodigious farming area.

20-21 • The Colorado River seen from Grand View Point, Canyonlands National Park, Utah.

23 • The Grand Prismatic Hot Spring is one of the most impressive of more than 10,000 geothermal features in Wyoming's Yellowstone National Park.

28-29 • Snow blankets Utah's Bryce Canyon National Park, one of several national parks on the geologically unique and diverse Colorado Plateau.

30-31 • Taos Pueblo, an ancient adobe structure in Taos, New Mexico, is still home to a community of Native American Tiwa, or Taos people.

32-33 • Mohawk Trail in western Massachusetts is one of New England's favorite spots for viewing colorful fall foliage.

SEAS and SHORELINES

- South of San Francisco, California's Highway 1 twists, climbs and winds along the coast of Big Sur, offering spectacular ocean vistas at every turn.

INTRODUCTION Seas and Shorelines

THE OCEAN BEACHES OF THE UNITED STATES OFFER SOMETHING FOR EVERY VARIETY OF BEACHGOER. FROM THE ROUGH BUT FRIENDLY SURF OF THE ATLANTIC COAST TO THE PLACID WATERS OF THE GULF OF MEXICO TO THE CRASHING WAVES OF THE PACIFIC COAST, SUN WORSHIPPERS, FAMILIES ON VACATION OR SURFERS SCOUTING FOR THE NEXT BIG WAVE FIND THAT SOMEWHERE IN AMERICA, THERE IS A BEACH FOR THEM.

FROM COASTAL MAINE, WHERE COLD WAVES CRASH AGAINST ROCKY BEACHES SCATTERED WITH GIANT BOULDERS, TO BLUSTERY CAPE COD – A GREAT SPOT FOR WHALEWATCHING – AND ON TO THE CALM WATERS OF LONG ISLAND SOUND, THE NORTHERN ATLANTIC OCEAN HAS MANY PERSONALITIES. FAMILIES FLOCK IN THE SUMMERTIME TO THE

INTRODUCTION Seas and Shorelines

SHORES OF NEW JERSEY, DELAWARE, MARYLAND AND VIR-GINIA, WHERE SLEEPY LITTLE TOWNS COME TO LIFE FOR THEIR GUESTS, AND WOODEN BOARDWALKS SPAN THE BEACHES. IN NORTH AND SOUTH CAROLINA, LIGHTHOUSES THAT ONCE PROTECTED SAILORS NOW SERVE AS PICTURESQUE SEN-TINELS ON WIDE, WHITE-SAND BEACHES WHERE THE SURF CAN RANGE FROM GENTLE TO ROUGH.

IN SOUTH FLORIDA, FORT LAUDERDALE AND MIAMI BEACH STILL DRAW THRONGS OF COLLEGE STUDENTS ON SPRING BREAK, "SNOWBIRDS" (PART-TIME WINTER RESIDENTS), SUPER-MODELS AND FILM CREWS TO THIS GLITZY COAST. A DECIDED-LY DIFFERENT MOOD PREVAILS IN THE FLORIDA KEYS, WHERE SPORT FISHING, BOATING, SNORKELING AND SCUBA DIVING COMPLEMENT THE LAID-BACK ISLAND ATTITUDE.

INTRODUCTION Seas and Shorelines

THE GULF OF MEXICO BORDERS FIVE U.S. STATES, AND PAR-
TICULARLY FUELS THE TOURISM ECONOMY OF WESTERN
FLORIDA. KNOWN FOR THEIR WHITE "SUGAR SAND," THE
BEACHES OF THE GULF COAST ARE CONSISTENTLY NAMED
AMONG THE WORLD'S MOST BEAUTIFUL. COASTAL WETLANDS
ALONG THE ENTIRE GULF OF MEXICO SUPPORT COUNTLESS
VARIETIES OF WILD ANIMALS, AND PROVIDE NEEDED BUFFERS
DURING HURRICANE SEASON.

THE PACIFIC OCEAN FROM WASHINGTON STATE TO CEN-
TRAL CALIFORNIA MAY BE TOO ROUGH AND COLD FOR SWIM-
MING, BUT THE SCENERY IS DRAMATIC AND BREATHTAKING. AT
SPOTS LIKE BIG SUR, GIANT WAVES CRASH AGAINST ROCKY
SHORES, SEA LIONS AND SHORE BIRDS RELAX ON OFFSHORE
ISLANDS, WILDFLOWERS AND TREES CLING TO LIFE ON SHEER

INTRODUCTION Seas and Shorelines

CLIFF FACES, AND THE ROLLING FIELDS AND FORESTS HALT ABRUPTLY TO GIVE WAY TO THE MIGHTY OCEAN BELOW. WHERE SWIMMERS DON'T DARE VENTURE, SURFERS CLAD IN WETSUITS PLY THE WATERS, PATIENTLY WAITING TO CONQUER THE NEXT BIG WAVE. THE MOST FAMOUS SURFING SPOT ON THE U.S. MAINLAND IS MAVERICKS NEAR HALF MOON BAY, CALIFORNIA. HERE WAVES OF MORE THAN 25 FEET (8 M) – SOMETIMES AS MUCH AS 50 FEET (15 M) – CHALLENGE THE WORLD'S MOST EXPERIENCED SURFERS.

SOUTHERN CALIFORNIA OFFERS SHORES MORE HOSPITABLE TO SUNBATHERS, WITH ICONIC LOCALES SUCH AS MALIBU AND VENICE BEACHES, AS WELL AS THE PRISTINE BEACHES OF DOZENS OF NATIONAL AND STATE PARKS AND THE CHANNEL ISLANDS.

Seas and Shorelines

Introduction

PERHAPS AMERICA'S MOST SOUGHT-AFTER BEACHES ARE THOSE FARTHEST FROM HER CONTINENTAL SHORES. THE HAWAIIAN ISLANDS SIT LIKE ROUGH-CUT EMERALDS MORE THAN 2,500 MILES (4,023 KM) FROM THE CONTINENTAL UNITED STATES. WITH ACTIVE VOLCANOES, DENSE RAINFORESTS, TURQUOISE WATERS AND A YEAR-ROUND BALMY CLIMATE, IT'S NO EXAGGERATION TO CALL HAWAII A TROPICAL PARADISE.

WINDY AND WILD. SUNNY AND CALM. COLD AND ROCKY. THOSE WHO ANSWER THE SIREN SONG OF THE OCEAN FIND THAT IN THE U.S.A., IT SINGS WITH MANY VOICES.

- The Point Vicente Lighthouse steers sailors clear of the rocky shoals at the northern end of the Catalina Channel in Southern California.

42 • Waves crash against the rough cliffs of Hanauma Bay, Oahu, Hawaii.

42-43 • The sheer volcanic cliffs of the Napali Coast on Kauai, the oldest of the Hawaiian Islands, make the region accessible only by foot or boat.

44-45 • The Kilauea Volcano on Hawaii's Big Island, is one of the most active volcanoes in the world.

46-47 • Sea kayaking is one of the many popular outdoor activities in the Hawaiian Islands, as are swimming, snorkeling, scuba diving, and surfing.

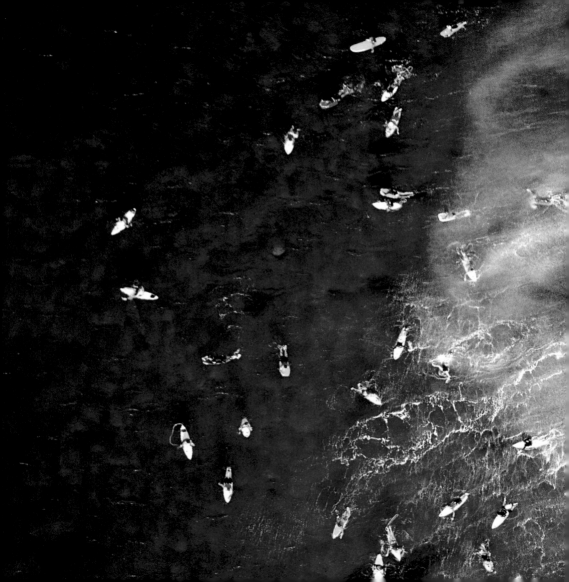

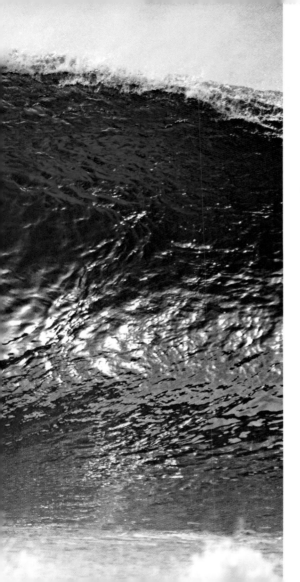

48-49 • Only experienced surfers tackle the Banzai Pipeline on the North Shore of Oahu, Hawaii, one of the world's most famous surfing sites, known for its tubular "pipe" waves.

49 • Summertime in Waimea Bay on Oahu along Hawaii's North Coast offers calm surf for swimmers, but in wintertime, it is the domain of surfboarders.

50-51 ● In the Pacific Ocean off the coast of Alaska, a pod of Humpback Whales feeds on herring using a "bubble net," a circle of bubbles blown by the group of whales to contain the small fish.

51 ● In what is thought to be part of a courtship ritual, a Humpback Whale breaches off the coast of Alaska.

● Accessible only by boat or small airplane, Glacier Bay National Park and Preserve, located near Juneau, Alaska, is home to a diverse array of wildlife, as well as glaciers that regularly "calve" or shed large junks of glacial ice into Glacier Bay.

A whale's tail breaks the surface of a calm glacial bay in the Inside Passage, the 500 miles (800 km) of protected coves and bays in Alaska's Alexander Archipelago.

A windsurfer carries his board across the sands of Oregon Dunes National Recreation Area, a 40-mile (64 km) stretch of protected coastal dunes, the largest in North America.

58-59 ● Tidepools at Seal Rock, Oregon support a unique variety of small marine life, while seals and sea lions frequently rest on the large rocks offshore.

60-61 ● The coastline of California's Big Sur region offers dramatic panoramas at every turn. The name loosely translates from the Spanish for "big south."

62 • Inhabited only by a few park rangers, Anacapa Island off the coast of Ventura, California, is the smallest of the northern Channel Islands.

63 • To protect the habitat of several rare and endangered species, day hikes and restricted primitive camping are among the limited human activities on Santa Cruz Island in California's Channel Islands.

64-65 • The sun sets on Catalina Harbor at Avalon, Santa Catalina Island, California. Catalina, as it is commonly known, is 22 miles off the coast of Los Angeles and has the largest year-round population of any of the Channel Islands.

● Jekyll Island, Georgia, at sunset. One of Georgia's four barrier islands accessible by car, Jekyll Island is a popular vacation destination for families and honeymooners.

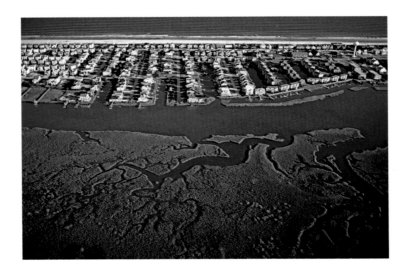

68 • Waterfront housing at Myrtle Beach, part of South Carolina's "Grand Strand" of barrier island beach resorts.

69 • The 1876 Morris Island Light once stood on dry land, but thanks to erosion at the mouth of South Carolina's Charleston Harbor, the lighthouse is now completely surrounded by water.

70-71 • Since 1879, Maine's picturesque Cape Neddick Lighthouse has warned passing ships with both a flashing light and a foghorn. The lighthouse and keeper's quarters sit on The Nubble, a rocky island at the mouth of the York River.

71 • Waves crash near Thunder Hole, Acadia National Park, Maine.

72-73 • Several small islands and waterfront fishing and lobstering villages are surrounded by Acadia National Park, Maine, the U.S.A.'s first national park east of the Mississippi.

74-75 ● Though the shifting sands and destructive winter hurricanes of the Atlantic Coast's barrier islands often claim beachfront houses such as these, the lure of life in close proximity to the ocean prompts many to rebuild.

76-77 ● Lobster, fishing and pleasure boats moor in the protected harbor of Perkin's Cove at Ogunquit, Maine. The Cove is a summertime tourist destination, with unique shops, cafes and galleries.

- Natural beauty, plus some of the most expensive real estate in the U.S.A. enhance a drive along Newport, Rhode Island's Ocean Drive, where Gilded Age mansions still house some of America's wealthiest "old money" families.

An offshore reef protects the shores of Palm Beach Island, an affluent community on Florida's southeast coast that lures jetsetters and everyday tourists alike.

Though most of the mid-20th century wooden homes were destroyed by Hurricane Andrew in 1992, a few remnants of "Stiltsville" remain in Florida's Biscayne National Park near Miami.

84-85 • A powerboat navigates the channels of Upper Matecumbe Key in the Florida Keys an archipelago of more than 1,700 islands, of which less than 50 are inhabited. A single highway connects the Keys to the Florida mainland.

86-87 • The calm, clear waters of the Florida Keys attract sun worshipers and sport fishermen alike. The waters surrounding the Keys, on both the Atlantic and Gulf of Mexico coasts, are all part of the Florida Keys National Marine Sanctuary.

MOUNTAINS' MAJESTY

• The Alaska Range in Denali National Park. The picturesque range is home to some of the harshest winter weather in the world.

INTRODUCTION Mountains Majesty

THE MOUNTAIN RANGES OF THE UNITED STATES ARE AS DIVERSE AS THE NATION ITSELF, FROM THE VERDANT, INVITING, RELATIVELY LOW PEAKS OF THE APPALACHIANS TO THE SEEMINGLY INSURMOUNTABLE HEIGHTS OF THE ROCKIES, AND WESTWARD STILL TO THE PERILOUS, SNOWBOUND TITANS OF ALASKA. IN PART BECAUSE OF THEIR INACCESSIBILITY AND IN PART BECAUSE OF A CONCERTED EFFORT TO PRESERVE THESE LIVING MONUMENTS, THE MOUNTAINS OF THE U.S.A. REMAIN SOME OF THE MOST PRISTINE, PROTECTED AREAS OF THE COUNTRY – DOTTED WITH NATIONAL PARKS AND FORESTS SUITABLE FOR DAY-TRIPPERS, AND FARTHER WEST, HOME TO VAST TRACTS OF UNTOUCHED WILDERNESS WHERE ELK, BEARS, WOLVES, FOXES AND OTHER MAMMALS FAR OUTNUMBER HUMANS.

THOUGH IT ORIGINATES IN CANADA, THE APPALACHIAN MOUN-

INTRODUCTION Mountains Majesty

TAIN CHAIN FIRST RISES IN THE U.S.A. IN NEW ENGLAND, WHERE IT STRADDLES MAINE, NEW HAMPSHIRE AND VERMONT AS IT BEGINS ITS 1,500-MILE MEANDER THROUGH THE EASTERN UNITED STATES, CULMINATING IN NORTHERN ALABAMA. IN COASTAL MAINE, THE NORTHERN APPALACHIANS TUMBLE INTO THE ATLANTIC ALONG ROCKY BEACHES AND CRAGGY CLIFFS. THE GREEN MOUNTAINS OF VERMONT AND THE WHITE MOUNTAINS OF NEW HAMPSHIRE PROVIDE BREATHTAKING SCENERY AND FOUR SEASONS OF BEAU-TY AND ENJOYMENT TO VISITORS AND RESIDENTS. FARTHER SOUTH, THE APPALACHIANS FORM THE SHENANDOAH AND BLUE RIDGE MOUNTAINS THROUGH VIRGINIA AND NORTH CAROLINA. THIS REGION OF THE APPALACHIANS IS PERHAPS THE MOST VISIT-ED, AS SKYLINE DRIVE IN VIRGINIA AND THE BLUE RIDGE PARKWAY TO ITS SOUTH OFFER MORE THAN 500 MILES OF VIRTUALLY UNIN-

INTRODUCTION Mountains Majesty

TERRUPTED, LOW-SPEED SCENIC ROADWAY. TO FIND THE NEXT
MOUNTAIN RANGE IN THE UNITED STATES WE MUST TRAVERSE
THOUSANDS OF MILES, TO WHERE THE GREAT PLAINS OF THE MID-
WEST GIVE WAY, DRAMATICALLY AND ABRUPTLY, TO THE STUN-
NING PEAKS OF THE ROCKY MOUNTAINS. THE ROCKIES, AS THEY
ARE POPULARLY KNOWN, EXTEND SOME 3,000 MILES FROM UP-
PERMOST CANADA TO NEW MEXICO IN THE SOUTHWESTERN
U.S.A. THE CONTINENTAL DIVIDE RUNS DOWN THE MIDDLE OF THE
ROCKIES. ALL RIVERS AND LAKES EAST OF THE DIVIDE DRAIN INTO
THE ATLANTIC OCEAN AND GULF OF MEXICO; THOSE WEST OF THE
DIVIDE DRAIN INTO THE PACIFIC. VAST TRACTS OF THE ROCKIES
ARE PRESERVED IN SOME OF AMERICA'S BEST-KNOWN AND MOST
SPECTACULAR NATIONAL PARKS, INCLUDING ROCKY MOUNTAIN
NATIONAL PARK IN COLORADO, AND YELLOWSTONE AND GRAND

INTRODUCTION Mountains Majesty

TETON IN WYOMING. THE CASCADE MOUNTAINS EXTEND THROUGH WASHINGTON, OREGON AND NORTHERN CALIFORNIA, AND THE TALLEST PEAKS OF THE CASCADES – INCLUDING MOUNT SHASTA IN CALIFORNIA, MOUNT HOOD IN OREGON, AND MOUNT RAINIER, MOUNT BAKER AND MOUNT ST. HELEN'S IN WASHINGTON – DOMINATE THEIR LANDSCAPES FOR MILES. THE CASCADES ARE ALSO HOME TO MANY OF THE UNITED STATES' DORMANT AND AC-TIVE VOLCANOES – 14 IN ALL – AS EVIDENCED BY THE DRAMATIC AND DESTRUCTIVE 1980 ERUPTION OF MOUNT ST. HELEN'S.

THE GEOLOGICAL DRAMA CONTINUES OUTSIDE THE CONTI-NENTAL U.S.A., WHERE ALASKA AND HAWAII OFFER MOUNTAIN RANGES IN STARK CONTRAST TO ONE ANOTHER. ALASKA'S MOUNT MCKINLEY (OR DENALI, ITS NATIVE AMERICAN NAME), IS THE UNITED STATES' TALLEST PEAK AT 20,335 FEET (6,198 M), AND

Mountains Majesty

Introduction

IS A SIREN CALL AND POTENTIALLY DEADLY RISK FOR EVEN THE MOST EXPERIENCED CLIMBERS. THE MOUNTAINS OF HAWAII, THOUGH OF LOWER ELEVATION, ARE NO LESS DRAMATIC, AS THEY RISE OUT OF THE CRASHING ULTRAMARINE WAVES OF THE PACIFIC OCEAN, TOWERING SENTINELS CLOAKED IN LUSH TROPICAL RAINFORESTS.

THE MOUNTAINS OF AMERICA, FROM SEA TO SEA, HAVE INSPIRED AWE, DISCOVERY AND INGENUITY. THEY'VE BEEN THE CHALLENGE AND THE NEMESIS OF EXPLORERS AND SETTLERS, THE CRADLE OF LIFE FOR NATIVE AMERICANS AND COUNTLESS SPECIES OF ANIMALS, AND ULTIMATELY, THE SOURCE OF ENDLESS BEAUTY AND WONDER FOR ALL WHO GAZE UPON THEM.

- In all four seasons, the Maroon Bells of the Rocky Mountains cast a perfect reflection in the waters of Maroon Lake.

96-97 ● On the Big Island of Hawaii, Volcanoes National Park is home to the longest continuously erupting volcano in the world. The molten rock rises from 60-70 miles (97-113 km) below the ocean floor.

98-99 ● A slow-moving glacial icefield in Alaska seems to suggest a frozen superhighway.

100-101 and 101 • These peaks of the Alaska Range are viewable only from helicopter or small plane, or by extremely experienced and daring mountain climbers.

102-103 • Ruth Glacier in Alaska's Denali National Park sits below the summit of Mount McKinley (Denali) and moves at a rate of 3.3 feet (1 m) per day.

104-105 • Crenulated snow blankets one of the countless peaks in the Denali National Park.

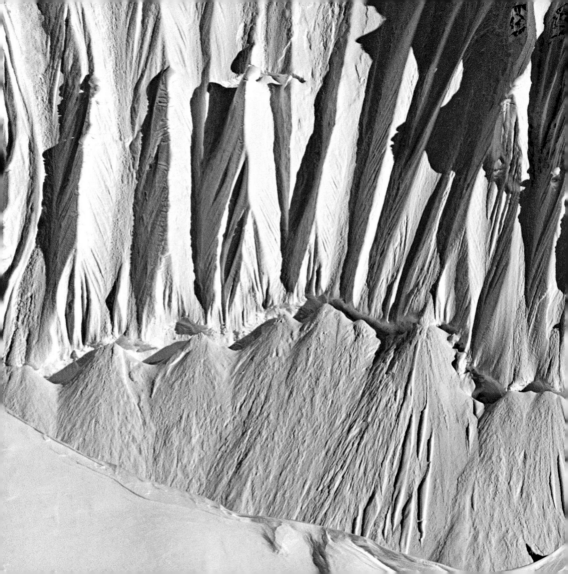

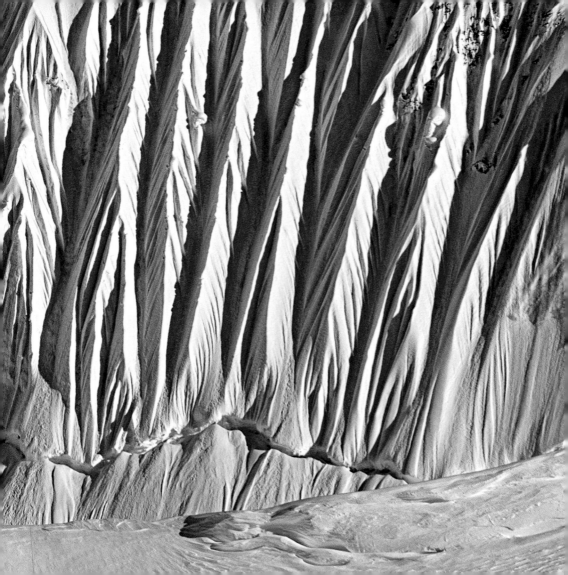

106-107 • At the height of winter, Alaska's Denali National Park sees only about five hours of daylight. Frigid temperatures ensure a deep snowpack from October to May.

108 • At 17,400 feet (5,304 m), Mount Foraker is 3,000 feet (914 m) shorter than its nearest neighbor, Mount McKinley (Denali). In the Native American language, the mountain is called "Menlale," which means "Denali's wife."

109 • Rugged Devil's Paw is the highest point in the Juneau Icefield. During winter storms, winds at the summit can top 200 miles per hour (322 kph).

110-111 • Denali National Park and Preserve protects 6 million acres of virtually uninterrupted wilderness, most of it inaccessible to humans.

112 • Shuksan in the Washington Cascades was formed by the collision of two gigantic land masses 120 million years ago.

113 • Ephemeral red alpenglow can often be seen at sunset or sunrise in the Cascade Range, Washington.

114-115 • The cone-shaped summit of Mount Saint Helens in Washington's Cascade Mountain Range was replaced by this mile-wide (1.6 km) crater when the volcano dramatically erupted in 1980.

116-117 • Though Mount Rainier in Washington's Cascade Mountain Range has been silent for more than 100 years, it is still an active volcano and has the potential to cause massive destruction and loss of life if it ever decides to erupt again. Mount Adams is in the distant background.

118-119 • Washington's Cascade Mountain Range receives one of the highest annual snowfalls in the world, up to 150 inches (3.8 m).

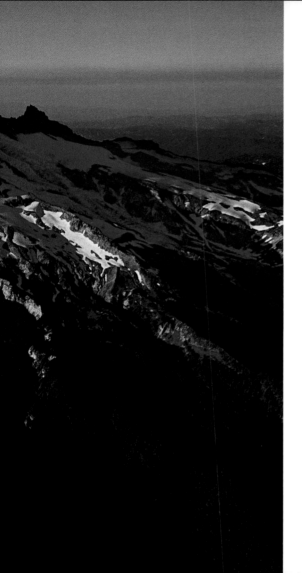

120-121 • The glaciated mountains of Olympic National Park in Washington are one of three distinct ecosystems in the park, which also contains a rugged coastline to the west, and to the east, a temperate rainforest.

121 • Nearly year-round cloudy conditions northwest of the Cascades make the peak of Mount Rainier a rare sight in Seattle, even though the 14,411-foot (4,392 m) mountain is just 54 miles (87 km) south of the city.

Twenty-five of an original 150 active glaciers remain at Glacier National Park, Montana, but these are threatened by rapid climate change, and may disappear as soon as 2030.

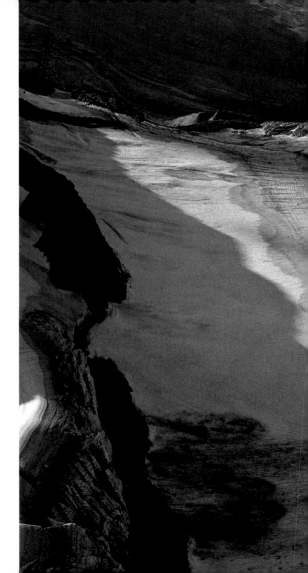

Though not as well known as neighboring Yellowstone National Park to its immediate north, Grand Teton National Park in Wyoming boasts higher peaks, popular with hikers and climbers.

A herd of wild horses still runs free at Grand Teton National Park, Wyoming. Originally brought to the Americas by the Spanish, wild horses are now a symbol of the American West.

128 • Mount Wilson, in Colorado's San Juan Mountains, is one of 53 "fourteeners" in Colorado – mountains more than 14,000 feet (4,267 m) above sea level. Dedicated mountaineers make it a goal to climb all of the state's tallest peaks.

129 • Though it wasn't named so for its million-dollar views, the Million Dollar Highway through the San Juan Mountains in Colorado affords drivers spectacular scenes at every turn, such as Mount Sneffels, another of Colorado's 14,000-foot peaks.

Center Peak is reflected in the cold, clear water of Golden Bear Lake, Kings Canyon National Park, California.

● A winter sunset in California's Yosemite National Park. Despite the snow cover that blankets most of Yosemite Valley from December through March, parts of the park remain open to visitors.

At 3,000 feet (914 m), El Capitan is the largest granite monolith in the world, and one of the most recognized features of Yosemite National Park. Hikers can make a gradual ascent up the back of El Capitan, while climbers challenge its sheer face.

Most visitors arrive at Thousand Island Lake on foot. Its remote location in California's Sierra Nevada mountain range ensures a peaceful spot for reading, resting, or simply taking in the lake's awesome natural beauty.

138 • An 11-mile (18 km) hiking trail leads to the summit of California's Mount Whitney, which at 14,505 feet (4,421 m) is the tallest peak in the continental United States.

138-139 • Near Mount Whitney, the Ritter Range is reflected in the waters of a high mountain lake.

140 and 140-141 • Though popular with day-trippers, hikers and campers, Sequoia and Kings Canyon National Parks, in California's Sierra Nevada mountains, still offer thousands of acres of remote wilderness to explore.

142-143 • The craggy peaks of high alpine country in Sequoia and Kings Canyon National Parks were shaped by glaciers. Much of California's Central Valley gets its water supply from the parks' watersheds.

144 and 144-145 • California's Yosemite National Park is one of the largest contiguous protected areas in the "lower 48" – the continental U.S.A., excluding Alaska.

146-147 • Named for the fog that often hangs over the rolling hills and pine forests, North Carolina's Great Smoky Mountains National Park is the most-visited national park in the United States.

UPTOWN
and DOWNTOWN

● Sunrise over the city that never sleeps. The Empire State Building towers over the Manhattan skyline, New York City, New York.

INTRODUCTION Uptown and Downtown

ARE THE HEART AND SPIRIT OF AMERICA FOUND IN ITS BUSTLING CITIES OR IN ITS FRIENDLY SMALL TOWNS? THE ANSWER IS YES. THE STORY OF THE UNITED STATES IS TOLD IN ITS FAST-PACED, CULTURED CITIES AS MUCH AS IN ITS LESSER-KNOWN POPULATION CENTERS, WHERE "MOM AND POP" BUSINESSES STILL THRIVE, AND WHERE PASSERSBY STILL STOP TO GREET ONE ANOTHER ON MAIN STREET.

ARGUABLY STILL THE MOST IMPORTANT CITY IN THE WORLD, NEW YORK – ACTUALLY A GROUP OF FIVE BOROUGHS OR DISTINCT DISTRICTS – IS A TRUE 24-HOUR CITY. AT ALL HOURS OF THE DAY AND NIGHT, TAXIS, BUSES, SUBWAY CARS AND EVEN FERRIES TRANSPORT THE CITY'S 8.4 MILLION RESIDENTS PAST DIZZYINGLY HIGH SKYSCRAPERS, OVER FAMOUS BRIDGES AND PAST ICONIC LANDMARKS

INTRODUCTION Uptown and Downtown

LIKE CENTRAL PARK, ROCKEFELLER CENTER AND THE STATUE OF LIBERTY.

LOCATED ABOUT FIVE HOURS FROM NEW YORK, BOSTON MANAGES TO BE A FULLY MODERN CITY WHILE STILL PRESERVING ITS HERITAGE AS THE BIRTHPLACE OF THE AMERICAN REVOLUTION. THE GREEN, LOW-RISE CITY OF WASHINGTON, D.C. IS EQUALLY RICH IN HISTORY – AND IT'S THE SEAT OF THE U.S GOVERNMENT, WHERE HISTORY IS MADE EVERY DAY.

NEARLY EVERY STATE IN AMERICA BOASTS A MAJOR CITY WITH ITS OWN UNIQUE CHARM AND PERSONALITY: MIAMI IS KNOWN FOR ITS DAZZLING BEACHES AND SIZZLING NIGHTLIFE. AMONG CHICAGO'S MANY CLAIMS TO FAME ARE ITS CLOUD-SCRAPING HIGH-RISES TOWERING OVER LAKE

INTRODUCTION Uptown and Downtown

MICHIGAN, AND ITS ROLE AS AMERICA'S THIRD MOST POPU-
LOUS CITY. ANY TEXAN WILL TELL YOU THAT FOLKS FROM
DALLAS, AMERICA'S FOURTH MOST POPULOUS CITY, ARE
FIERCELY INDEPENDENT AND PROUD OF THEIR SOUTH-
WESTERN ROOTS. THE UNITED STATES' SECOND LARGEST
CITY, LOS ANGELES, IS A VAST URBAN AREA, HOME TO THE
HOLLYWOOD FILM INDUSTRY, YEAR-ROUND PLEASANT
WEATHER AND A HUGE, DIVERSE IMMIGRANT POPULATION.
FARTHER NORTH, SAN FRANCISCO, BUILT INTO THE STEEP
HILLS OVER SAN FRANCISCO BAY, BOASTS A FREE-SPIRITED
VIBE AND A DEVIL-MAY-CARE ATTITUDE TOWARD THE CON-
STANT THREAT OF EARTHQUAKES. IN SEATTLE, ESPRESSO-
DRINKING RESIDENTS AND VISITORS WAIT FOR A RARE
CLEAR DAY TO CATCH A GLIMPSE OF MOUNT RAINIER.

INTRODUCTION Uptown and Downtown

YET IT'S NOT JUST DENSELY PACKED CITIES THAT CRE-
ATE THE CHARACTER OF THE U.S.A. IN THE SOUTH, HORSE-
DRAWN CARRIAGES STILL PLY THE TREE-SHADED COBBLE-
STONE STREETS OF SAVANNAH, GEORGIA AND ST. AUGUS-
TINE, FLORIDA, WHILE BLUES, BLUEGRASS AND COUNTRY
MUSIC LEGENDS – AND ASPIRING LEGENDS – PLAY TO
CROWDS IN NASHVILLE AND MEMPHIS. IN THE MIDWEST, ST.
LOUIS AND KANSAS CITY BORE WITNESS TO THE WEST-
WARD EXPANSION IN THE 19TH AND 20TH CENTURIES, AND
MUCH OF THE BRICK AND VICTORIAN ARCHITECTURE RE-
MAINS AS EVIDENCE OF THAT PERIOD. IN THE NORTHERN
MIDWEST CITIES OF THE GREAT LAKES, ETHNIC COMMUNI-
TIES AND REGIONAL ACCENTS AND CUISINE – AS WELL AS A
HARDY TOLERANCE FOR COLD WEATHER – CONTRIBUTE

Uptown and Downtown
Introduction

SIGNIFICANTLY TO THE IDENTITIES OF DETROIT, MILWAUKEE AND A HOST OF SMALLER CITIES. IN THE SOUTHWEST, SPANISH, MEXICAN AND NATIVE AMERICAN INFLUENCES ARE STRONGLY FELT IN THE DESERT CITIES OF SANTA FE, TUCSON AND ALBUQUERQUE.

IT WOULD TAKE MONTHS TO VISIT ALL OF AMERICA'S STATE CAPITALS, AND MANY MORE TO SEE ITS MANY FASCINATING CITIES AND TOWNS. CULTURALLY AND ETHNICALLY DIVERSE, WITH DISTINCT CUISINES, CUSTOMS AND PERSONALITIES, THE GREAT QUILT OF THE UNITED STATES IS COMPOSED OF MANY FABRICS, AND EVERY DOT ON THE MAP, LARGE OR SMALL, IS AN ESSENTIAL STITCH IN THAT QUILT.

● An iconic streetcar surmounts Nob Hill, with the Bay Bridge in the background, San Francisco, California.

The Diamond Head volcanic crater looms over the city of Honolulu, Hawaii, and is a popular hiking spot for tourists and residents alike.

158-159 and 159 ● Seattle, Washington's setting between the Pacific Ocean and the Cascade Mountain Range provides for year-round outdoor pursuits, as well as an abundance of rain. At left, the Space Needle, built for the 1962 World's Fair and now a symbol of Seattle.

160-161 ● Seattle's Lake Union is home to an entire neighborhood of houseboats, floating residences that truly epitomize "waterfront living."

162-163 • The Golden Gate Bridge is the symbol of San Francisco, and one of the most recognized structures in the world. It was the longest-span suspension bridge in the world when it opened in 1937.

164-165 • San Francisco's Financial District, with the Transamerica Pyramid at left.

• Fisherman's Wharf (top) and the San
Francisco Maritime National Historical
Park (right) are popular attractions that
preserve the city's waterfront culture.
At right, Coit Tower sits atop Telegraph Hill.

168 and 169 • Los Angeles, California. Sunset Boulevard (bottom) lures tourists and countless aspiring movie stars in search of fame and fortune, or just a celebrity autograph, to LA, as it is commonly known. Just don't make a wrong turn on one of the city's mazelike freeway interchanges (right).

170-171 • Downtown Los Angeles, California. The second-most populous city in the U.S.A., the greater LA region is home to an amazing array of diverse neighborhoods and cultures.

172-173 • Passersby seem to blend in effortlessly with a mural in downtown Santa Monica, an oceanfront community in Los Angeles County, California.

173 • More than 200 Hollywood stars have left their foot- and handprints in the sidewalk outside Grauman's Chinese Theatre on Hollywood Boulevard, Hollywood, California.

174 ● The Frank Gehry-designed Walt Disney Concert Hall is a modern icon in downtown Los Angeles.

174-175 ● The setting sun lights up the skyscrapers of downtown LA, and aptly reflects Los Angeles' reputation as a glittering city of possibilities.

California's southernmost major city, San Diego is noted for its year-round sunny weather, abundant beaches and Spanish-influenced architecture.

178 ● The Stratosphere Tower looms over "The Strip," Las Vegas' main artery. In the image: Hotels and casinos along The Strip vie for tourist dollars.

178-179 ● Perhaps no city in the world reflects the human desire to manipulate the environment so much as Las Vegas, a dazzling manmade entertainment palace.

180-181 • Only in Las Vegas. Cannonballs and musket-fire echo nightly at Las Vegas' Treasure Island Hotel and Casino, when marauding "pirates" put on free shows.

182 and 182-183 • Arthurian legend lives on at the castle-like Excalibur Hotel and Casino, top, while New York City – complete with rollercoaster – is the draw at the New York, New York Hotel and Casino, both in Las Vegas.

For 19th century American pioneers heading west, Kansas City, Missouri was the last major stopover before the long westward journey. Its position on the Missouri River made it an important shipping and trading post.

On the Mississippi River, St. Louis, Missouri's best-known landmark is the famous Gateway Arch, designed by Eero Saarinen and built to commemorate St. Louis' role as the "Gateway to the West" during the United States' westward expansion.

188-189 ● The oil and cotton industries built Dallas, Texas, now America's ninth largest city and a major commercial center in the South.

190-191 ● Though Dallas, Texas, has several historic neighborhoods that reflect its 19th century roots, its skyline is shaped by the daring modern and postmodern architecture of the late 20th century.

192 • The Bank of America Center looms over Minute Maid Park, home of the Houston (Texas) Astros baseball team.

193 • A Jean Dubuffet sculpture under Houston's Wells Fargo Plaza, the world's tallest all-glass building.

194-195 ● The 100-year-old Navy Pier on Lake Michigan is no longer used for military operations and is now a major entertainment destination in Chicago, Illinois.

196-197 ● The Great Chicago Fire of 1871 left downtown Chicago in ruins, and ushered in a remarkable period of innovative construction known as the "Skyscraper Era." Today, the Chicago skyline is a mix of some of the U.S.A.'s oldest major skyscrapers and some of its newest.

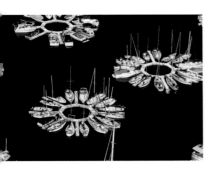

198 • Sailboats cluster around floating docks in Chicago's Lake Michigan.

198-199 • In Chicago, even parking garages are in skyscrapers at Marina City, the U.S.A.'s first post-WWII high-rise residential complex.

Opened in 1995, the Rock and Roll Hall of Fame (the white building at center left) on Lake Erie helped jumpstart a renaissance of the downtown waterfront in Cleveland, Ohio.

• Once a center for the slave and cotton trades and later a hotbed of the 1960s Civil Rights Movement, Memphis, Tennessee, is better known today as the home of blues music, as heard on historic Beale Street (right).

204-205 ● The twin span Crescent City Connection, formerly known as the Greater New Orleans Bridge, carries eight lanes of traffic across the Mississippi River in New Orleans.

205 ● New Orleans' most famous 14 blocks, Bourbon Street runs the length of the French Quarter, where charming, historic architecture meets raucous nightlife.

206 • Though the city had modest beginnings in the 19th century, today Atlanta, Georgia is the most populous city in the U.S. South, and is home to several Fortune 500 companies, and corporate giants such as Coca-Cola, CNN, and Delta Airlines.

207 • Suntrust Plaza, a multiuse commercial complex in downtown Atlanta.

208-209 • Waterfront property is a hot commodity in Florida, so much so that countless neighborhoods such as this, built on artificial islands, line both coasts of the Florida peninsula.

● Daytona Beach on Florida's Atlantic Coast has long been a vacation destination for families and college "spring breakers." Top: A bridge connects the mainland to sandy beaches lined with hotels and condominiums.

Orlando, Florida is famous for its several major theme parks. Top left: Sea World, a marine mammal park. Top right: Walt Disney World's Magic Kingdom. Right: Cinderella's Castle at Disney's Magic Kingdom, one of six Disney theme parks in the Orlando-Kissimmee area of central Florida.

An international flavor, an enviable oceanfront location and year-round warm weather are all part of the lure of Miami, Florida. Here, modern downtown Miami rises over the protected waters of Biscayne Bay.

216 • Waterfront estates line the shores of a Miami waterway.

217 • Once a sleepy retirement destination for Northerners, Miami Beach is now an international hotspot, attracting models, singers and celebrities to its vibrant nightlife and luxury hotels and residences.

218 • The White House, at 1600 Pennsylvania Avenue, Washington, D.C., has been the home of every U.S. President since John Adams.

219 • Just up the street from the White House, the U.S. Capitol is home to the Congress, the legislative branch of government comprising the Senate and the House of Representatives.

220-221 ● The National Mall in Washington, D.C. is a multiacre public park lined with major museums and monuments, like the Lincoln Memorial (foreground) and the world's tallest obelisk, the 555-foot (169 m) Washington Monument.

221 ● Adjacent to the National Mall is the Jefferson Memorial, built to honor the third President of the United States, Thomas Jefferson.

The Brown Memorial Park Avenue Presbyterian Church, with its neo-Gothic spires and domes and eleven original Tiffany stained-glass windows, is one of Baltimore, Maryland's most significant structures.

Old and new meld in Philadelphia, Pennsylvania. Modern One Liberty Place (top) rises above a city that was key to the founding of the United States. Thomas Paine Plaza (right) pays tribute to some of America's founding fathers.

BENJAMIN FRANKLIN - CRAFTSMAN

Four clocks, each 26 feet (8 m) in diameter adorn the face of Philadelphia's City Hall, the second tallest masonry building in the world.

The incomparable skyline of Manhattan, New York City, home to 1.6 million people, 13,000 taxicabs and more than 3,000 hot dog stands.

230 and 230-231 • Central Park, the most-visited city park in the U.S.A., reveals a quieter side of New York City. Bottom: The Bethesda Fountain framed by fall color. Right: The 1896 Gapstow Bridge, spanning the Central Park Pond.

232-233 • In good weather, a center walkway on New York's Brooklyn Bridge, which connects the island of Manhattan to the borough of Brooklyn, attracts walkers, joggers and bicyclists.

Although early 20th century immigrants to the United States stopped at Ellis Island for processing, Liberty Island and the Statue of Liberty were the first things newcomers saw as they approached New York City. "Lady Liberty" as she is affectionately known, has come to symbolize the hope and promise of America.

236-237 • Trumpeting angels, a 75-year old live Christmas tree and a bronze statue of the Greek god Prometheus greet holiday visitors to New York City's Rockefeller Center.

238-239 • At 102 stories tall, the Empire State Building is New York City's tallest structure.

240-241 • Exclusive Newport, Rhode Island is famous as a summer retreat for wealthy New Englanders and as the sailing capital of the United States.

242-243 • The Longfellow Bridge spans the Back Bay in Boston, Massachusetts.

INTO the HEARTLAND

- A grain elevator surrounded by fields of freshly-harvested wheat, Oregon.

INTRODUCTION Into the Heartland

THE IDEA OF THE AMERICAN FARM CONJURES A NORMAN ROCKWELL-LIKE IMAGE OF A HARDWORKING FAMILY GATHERED AROUND THE DINNER TABLE AFTER A LONG DAY'S WORK IN THE FIELDS. THEY DINE ON THE FRUITS OF THEIR LABOR, TIRED BUT SATISFIED WITH THE LIFE FARMING AFFORDS THEM. THOUGH THIS IS LARGELY A NOSTALGIC SCENE FROM A BYGONE ERA, AND FARMING IN THE UNITED STATES HAS CHANGED RADICALLY IN THE LAST CENTURY, AGRICULTURE IS STILL A DRIVING ECONOMIC FORCE. THE U.S.A. GROWS NEARLY 50 PERCENT OF THE WORLD'S GRAIN SUPPLY, AND ANNUALLY EXPORTS BILLIONS OF BUSHELS OF CORN, SOYBEANS, WHEAT AND OTHER FOOD CROPS. LIVESTOCK IS ANOTHER IMPORTANT FARMING INDUSTRY IN THE U.S.A., AS THE DAIRY PRODUCTS, BEEF, PORK AND POULTRY THAT ARRIVE AT AMERICAN TABLES

ARE ALMOST ALL PRODUCED WITHIN HER BORDERS.

DIFFERENT REGIONS OF AMERICA ARE DISTINGUISHED BY THEIR AGRICULTURAL OUTPUT. FOR EXAMPLE, FLORIDA IS AS-SOCIATED WITH CITRUS: GROWING ORANGES, GRAPEFRUIT AND TANGERINES IS A MAJOR INDUSTRY IN THE "SUNSHINE STATE," WHICH ALSO PRODUCES BOUNTIFUL CROPS OF STRAWBERRIES. THOUGH THE REGAL PLANTATION HOUSES OF GEORGIA (THE "PEACH STATE") AND OTHER PARTS OF THE DEEP SOUTH ARE RELICS OF THE 19TH CENTURY, COTTON, PEACHES, PEANUTS AND TOBACCO FARMS STILL THRIVE. THE MIDWEST IS HOME TO HUGE LIVESTOCK HERDS AND ENDLESS ROWS OF CORN, WHEAT, SUNFLOWERS, SORGHUM AND SOY (KANSAS IS THE "SUNFLOWER STATE"; NEBRASKA, THE "CORN-HUSKER STATE"). HEAD TO WISCONSIN FOR CHEESE AND OTH-

INTRODUCTION Into the Heartland

ER DAIRY PRODUCTS, TO SOUTHERN CALIFORNIA FOR CAN-
TALOUPES, OLIVES AND ALMONDS.

MANY REGIONS OF THE UNITED STATES ARE RENOWNED
FOR THE HIGH QUALITY OF THEIR SPECIALTY AGRICULTURAL
PRODUCTS. NEW ENGLAND TREATS US TO PURE MAPLE SYRUP
TAPPED RIGHT FROM THE TREE TRUNK, SHARP CHEDDAR
CHEESE AND TANGY CRANBERRIES. THANKS TO THE MEDITER-
RANEAN-LIKE CLIMATE OF NAPA AND SONOMA VALLEYS, CALI-
FORNIA WINERIES NOW COMPETE WITH THE FINEST VINTAGES
OF FRANCE AND ITALY. OREGON AND WASHINGTON ALSO PRO-
DUCE FINE WINES, AND ARE ESPECIALLY NOTED FOR THEIR
PINOT NOIRS. IN AUTUMN, FRESH, CRISP WASHINGTON APPLES
ARRIVE IN SUPERMARKETS ACROSS THE COUNTRY. IN THE UP-
PER MIDWEST, MICHIGAN CLAIMS THE TITLE "CHERRY CAPITAL

INTRODUCTION Into the Heartland

OF THE WORLD" AND CELEBRATES BOTH SWEET AND TART VARIETIES OF THE FRUIT WITH AN ANNUAL CHERRY FESTIVAL. ROWS AND ROWS OF LOW-GROWING PINEAPPLE PLANTS COVER THE HILLY VOLCANIC LANDSCAPE OF HAWAII, WHICH IS REPUTED TO PRODUCE SOME OF THE WORLD'S SWEETEST OF THE FUNNY-LOOKING FRUIT.

BUT NOT ALL AGRICULTURE IN THE U.S.A. IS INTENDED FOR DINNER TABLES. COTTON IS STILL KING IN TEXAS, THE NATION'S LARGEST PRODUCER OF THE UTILITARIAN FIBER. EVERY YEAR, 70 MILLION CHRISTMAS TREE SEEDLINGS – MOSTLY SCOTCH PINE AND FIR VARIETIES – ARE PLANTED IN STATES ACROSS THE COUNTRY. FOR BETTER OR WORSE, TOBACCO FARMING IS STILL A MAJOR INDUSTRY IN NORTH CAROLINA, KENTUCKY, TENNESSEE, AND SEVERAL OTHER SOUTHERN AND MID-AT-

Into the Heartland
Introduction

LANTIC STATES. FIFTEEN STATES, LED BY CALIFORNIA, FLORIDA AND HAWAII, PRODUCE 75 PERCENT OF ALL CUT FLOWERS, POTTED PLANTS AND GARDEN FOLIAGE SOLD IN THE U.S.A.

STILL, AMERICAN FARMS PROVIDE MUCH MORE THAN FOOD, DRINK, FUEL AND CLOTHING. THEIR ROLLING, MULTICOLORED FIELDS, IN A RANGE OF HUES FROM GOLDEN TO BRILLIANT YEL-LOWS, VERDANT GREENS TO VIBRANT REDS, ARE AN ENDLESS DELIGHT TO BEHOLD. THEIR UBIQUITOUS RED BARNS ARE ICON-IC SYMBOLS OF OUR AGRICULTURAL HERITAGE. THEY ARE A LIVING REMINDER THAT WHEN WE TAKE CARE OF THE LAND, THE LAND TAKES CARE OF US, SHARING HER BEAUTY AND BOUNTY.

251 • A sod farm on the rich, hilly terrain of the Palouse Hills in eastern Washington.

252-253 • Pineapple plantations like the one pictured here in Oahu thrive in Hawaii's volcanic soil and tropical climate.

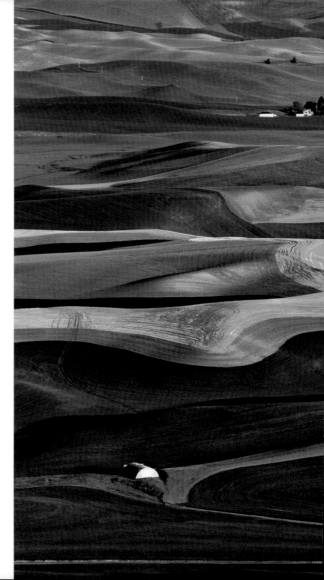

• The gentle, undulating hills of a large sod farm in Palouse County, eastern Washington.

From high overhead, rows of tulips form a geometric carpet in Washington's Skagit Valley.

● Springtime in the Hood River Valley, Oregon brings an explosion of pear blossoms in a commercial orchard.

Sugar beets, wheat and barley flourish in the high plains of Wyoming. Pictured top and right: A large-scale farming operation in Laramie County.

● A combine harvests
wheat in the semi-arid
eastern plains of Wyoming.

264 • Near Dodge City, Kansas, alfalfa is harvested and rolled into bales to use as feed for horses and cattle.

265 • Putah Creek winds through a patchwork of agricultural fields outside of Winters, California, just an hour away from San Francisco.

● It's not all about movie stars:
Top and right, the agricultural fields
of eastern Los Angeles County,
California, produce alfalfa, onions,
carrots, potatoes, peaches,
grapes and nectarines.

268 • Irrigation of the arid terrain makes citrus groves like these viable in the Anza Borrego Desert, California.

268-269 • Colorful mustard plants placed between rows of grapevines enrich soil and reduce erosion in California's Napa Valley vineyards.

270-271 • Though northern Californian wine is better known, the Santa Monica Mountains near Los Angeles are home to more than 50 vintners.

272-273 • Who says farming is all work and no play? Cornfield mazes, such as the one pictured above, are scattered throughout America's corn-growing states.

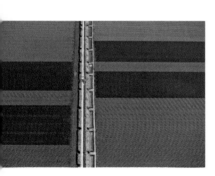

• Despite being one of the hottest cities in the U.S.A., Yuma, Arizona (top and right) is a major farming center, producing citrus, melons, leafy greens, corn and cotton. Piped-in irrigation, pictured above, makes it possible.

Though farming is now more mechanized than ever, the life of a farmer still means long hours of labor in the fields. Pictured here, a tractor cutting crops near Omaha, Nebraska.

The soils of eastern Colorado, drained by the neighboring Rocky Mountains, are some of the most fertile in the United States.

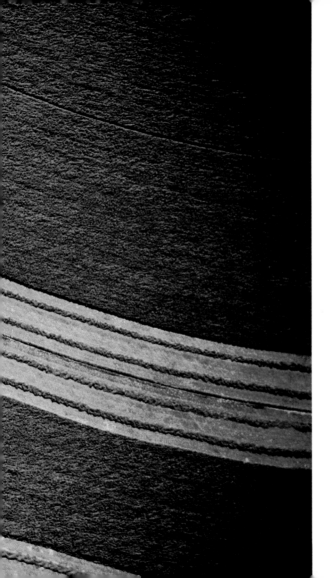

280-281 • The U.S.A. is the largest alfalfa producer in the world, with the majority of crops grown in California, South Dakota and Wisconsin.

282-283 • Running white fences stand out sharply against vibrant green pastures at a horse farm near Lexington, Kentucky, a world-renowned horse breeding region.

284-285 • Near Lake Champlain, Vermont, harvested pumpkins sit ready to be carved for Halloween.

Sunderland, a small farming community on the Connecticut River in Massachusetts, awash in fall color.

288-289 ● An antique wooden barn along the Mohawk Trail, once a Native American trade route and now a scenic highway in western Massachusetts.

289 ● A historic cottage at Crawford Notch, in the White Mountains of New Hampshire.

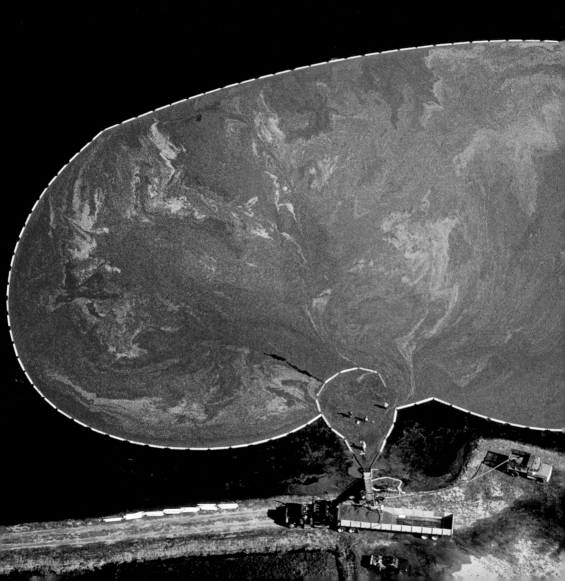

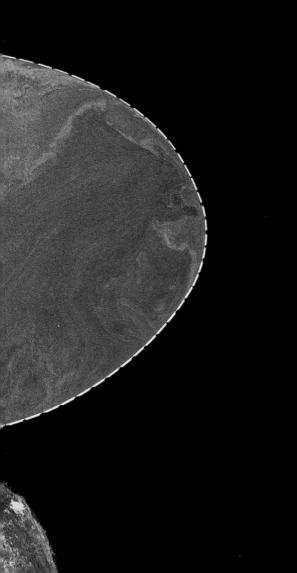

290-291 • Using a unique U.S. farming method, cranberries are grown in bogs, knee-deep ponds exactly suited to this tangy berry. At this Massachusetts bog, floating cranberries are corralled and loaded onto waiting trucks.

292-293 • The northeastern shoreline of the U.S.A. is home to the majority of the nation's cranberry cultivation. Pictured here, a cranberry bog at Carver, Massachusetts.

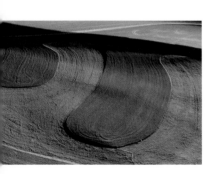

● When viewed from overhead, these fields in the Palouse Hills of Washington (top) and the eastern shore of Maryland (right) form a multicolored jigsaw puzzle.

296 and 296-297 ● The patterns created by these rolling rows of crops in North Carolina (bottom) and Washington state (right) take on an almost-meditative quality.

298-299 ● In central Florida, a tractor prepares raised soil beds for a new crop of strawberries. An important commercial crop in the state, Florida strawberries are also sold at "u-pick" farms, where visitors can pick their own to take home.

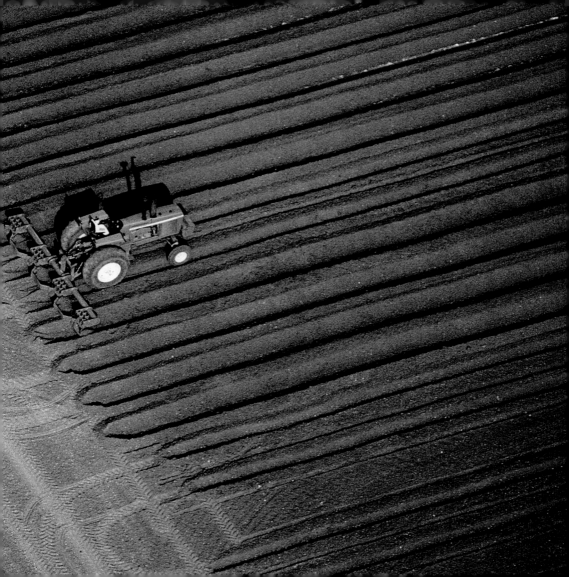

LIVING SANDS

Water, wind and time have carved these enigmatic sandstone formations in Monument Valley, a well-known feature of the Colorado Plateau, near the border of Arizona and Utah.

INTRODUCTION Living Sands

BELOW SEA LEVEL AT ITS LOWEST POINT) THE HIGHEST TEMPERA-
TURES (UP TO 134°F [56.7 °C]) AND THE DRIEST CONDITIONS (LESS
THAN 2 INCHES [50.8 MM] OF RAIN PER YEAR) OF ANYWHERE IN
THE U.S.A., STILL MANAGES TO SUPPORT MORE THAN 1,000 PLANT
SPECIES, 51 SPECIES OF MAMMALS, NEARLY 350 TYPES OF BIRDS
AND DOZENS OF SPECIES OF REPTILES, ALL OF WHICH HAVE
ADAPTED TO THIS SEEMINGLY INHOSPITABLE CLIMATE.

THE SONORAN DESERT ABUTS THE MOHAVE TO THE SOUTH,
COVERS MUCH OF SOUTHWESTERN ARIZONA AND CALIFORNIA
AND EXTENDS INTO MEXICO. THE SONORAN DESERT IS THE ONLY
PLACE IN THE WORLD WHERE THE ICONIC, MANY-ARMED
SAGUARO CACTUS GROWS. THE SLOW-GROWING SAGUARO HAS
AN EXTREMELY LONG LIFESPAN – THE OLDEST-KNOWN SPECIMEN
IS AT LEAST 150 YEARS OLD.

Living Sands

Introduction

SITTING ASTRIDE THE RIO GRANDE, WHICH FORMS THE NATU-
RAL BORDER BETWEEN MEXICO AND THE U.S.A., IS THE CHI-
HUAHUAN DESERT. WITH ITS VARIED ELEVATIONS AND HABITATS,
IT IS HOME TO LARGE MAMMALS SUCH AS BIG-HORNED SHEEP,
MULE DEER, MOUNTAIN LIONS AND BEARS, SMALLER COYOTES,
AND A RICH ARRAY OF REPTILES, BIRDS AND SMALL MAMMALS.

THE MARCH OF PROGRESS HAS BROUGHT PAVED ROADS,
GAS STATIONS, RESTAURANTS AND PARK RANGER STATIONS TO
THESE DESERT CLIMES, THUS REMOVING MANY OF THE DAN-
GERS OF DESERT TRAVEL. BUT A TRIP ACROSS ANY U.S. DESERT
CAN STILL TRANSPORT VISITORS BACK TO A TIME WHEN THE
AMERICAN WEST REALLY WAS A WILD PLACE.

- Though Death Valley in the Mohave Desert of California has actually claimed very few lives, it is one of the least hospitable places on Earth, at least for humans.

Stratified minerals create a colorful canvas in the exposed hills of Death Valley, California.

310-311 ● The view from Zabriskie Point, one of the many picturesque vantage points within Death Valley National Park, California.

312-313 ● The Mesquite Sand Dunes, pictured here near Stovepipe Wells, a small way-station within Death Valley National Park, have served as the setting for countless Western and science fiction films, including *Star Wars*.

314-315 ● A view of the "badlands" at Zabriskie Point, Death Valley National Park, so-named because the terrain is so difficult to cross on foot or horseback.

316-317 ● The colors of the Artist's Palette, Death Valley are caused by the oxidation of metals in the rock faces.

318-319 ● Joshua trees stand as lonely sentinels in front of the "Old Woman Rock," a popular climbing spot at Joshua Tree National Park, California.

Desert Agave flourishes in a low-lying area of Anza-Borrego Desert State Park, southern California.

322 and 322-323 • Bryce Canyon Amphitheater in Bryce Canyon National Park, Utah. The spectacular rock formations developed as a result of erosion by wind, ice and water in a process that began tens of millions of years ago.

324-325 • Despite its extreme age (65 million years), Bryce Canyon is the youngest member of the Grand Staircase, a vast geological zone formed by Bryce, Zion and Grand canyons.

326-327 ● Pinnacles, buttes and cliffs carved from red sandstone characterize the Valley of the Gods scenic area near Mexican Hat, Utah.

328-329 ● Delicate Arch in Arches National Park near Moab, Utah, is one of the most photographed formations in the park, and is the state symbol of Utah.

330 and 330-331 ● For at least 10,000 years, humans have visited the high desert area that is now Canyonlands National Park, Utah (right). Bottom: Some indigenous rock art predates European contact by at least 1,000 years.

332-333 ● One of the "meanders" of the San Juan River at Goosenecks State Park, near Moab, Utah. The rocks that form the river gorge are up to 300 million years old.

334-335 • Sunrise paints a brilliant palette in Arizona's Grand Canyon National Park, one of the United States' first, and now most visited national parks.

336-337 • The colorful, intensely stratified layers of the Grand Canyon expose two billion years of the Earth's geologic history. Even the youngest rocks in the canyon are a million years old.

338 and 338-339 • The Grand Canyon was formed by a massive rift in the Colorado Plateau, the geographic range that contains much of the desert area of the U.S.A. The Colorado River continues to carve its path on the canyon floor.

340-341 • "The Mittens," two strangely similar sandstone buttes, rise from the floor of Monument Valley. The valley lies within the Navajo Nation autonomous region, in Arizona and Utah.

Iron oxide provides the rich red color of Monument Valley. Here, a sand dune in the foreground, with the Totem Pole formation in the background.

● Sandstone buttes and pinnacles stand in clusters (top) and seem to march in silent unison (right) across the floor of Monument Valley.

Volcanic ash engulfed and petrified these 225-million-year-old trees, now the namesakes of Petrified Forest National Park near Navajo, Arizona.

Canyon de Chelly National
Monument, in eastern Arizona
near the New Mexico border,
is located entirely within the
Navajo Nation land trust.
Apart from its scenic beauty,
the canyon contains some
of the best-preserved ruins
of the Anasazi culture.

350 and 351 • Organ Pipe Cactus National Park in southern Arizona is home to the very rare Organ Pipe Cactus, pictured at right. The remote location of the park offers visitors vast panoramas uninterrupted by signs of human development.

352-353 • Saguaro cacti silhouetted against the sunset in Organ Pipe Cactus National Park, Arizona.

354-355 • The red rocks of Sedona, Arizona lure visitors, both for their dazzling beauty and their purported mystical properties. Cathedral Rock, pictured here, is said to be a center of spiritual energy.

356-357 ● Mesa Verde National Park, Colorado is best known for its spectacular Anasazi cliff dwellings, constructed around 1200 AD.

358-359 ● Great Sand Dunes National Park and Preserve, in eastern Colorado, contains the largest sand dunes in North America, with heights reaching 750 feet (229 m). The Sangre de Cristo mountain range towers in the background.

360-361 ● Hikers stand on the ridge of one of the constantly shifting dunes at Great Sand Dunes National Park and Preserve, Colorado.

362-363 ● At more than 1,580 feet (482 m) Shiprock is located within the Navajo Nation in the Four Corners region of New Mexico. For the Navajo and their Anasazi ancestors, it was and is a site of great spiritual importance.

364 and 364-365 • Only the hardiest of plants and animals have adapted to the harsh environment – extreme temperatures and very little water – of White Sands National Monument, in New Mexico's Chihuahuan Desert near the Texas border.

366-367 • White Sands National Monument is the world's largest gypsum dune area. The mineral is responsible for the desert's glistening white appearance.

368-369 • Badlands National Park in South Dakota has one of the world's richest fossil deposits.

MAJESTIC
WATERWAYS

The Colorado River winds through Cataract Canyon, part of Canyonlands National Park and Glen Canyon National Recreation Area, Utah.

INTRODUCTION Majestic Waterways

ACROSS THE UNITED STATES, A VAST NETWORK OF INTER-CONNECTING LAKES AND RIVERS HAVE FOR MILLENNIA PROVIDED WATER, FOOD, MEANS OF TRANSPORT AND PASSAGES TO UNCHARTED LANDS. THE WATERWAYS OF AMERICA HAVE GIVEN RISE TO NATIVE AMERICAN VILLAGES, THEN FRONTIER TRADING POSTS, THEN BUSTLING CITIES AND ULTIMATELY, METROPOLISES. BOTH VIOLENT AND PLACID, THE WATERWAYS HAVE THE POWER TO CARVE OUT CANYONS AND SINK SHIPS, OR GENTLY IRRIGATE FARM FIELDS AND LAP AT SANDY SHORES.

THE GRANDFATHER OF ALL AMERICAN RIVERS IS OF COURSE THE MISSISSIPPI, KNOWN AS "OLD MAN RIVER." HIS HEADWATERS SPRING INNOCUOUSLY FROM A LAKE IN NORTHERN MINNESOTA – AT A SHALLOW, 10 FOOT (3 M) WIDE STREAM THAT MARKS THE START OF THE RIVER'S 2,320-MILE (3,734-KM) JOURNEY TO THE

GULF OF MEXICO. KNOWN AS "BIG RIVER" OR "BIG MUDDY," THE MISSOURI RIVER ORIGINATES IN THE HIGH MOUNTAINS OF MONTANA AND MEANDERS SOUTHEAST TO MEET THE MISSISSIPPI. FARTHER NORTH AND EAST, THE OHIO RIVER MEETS THE MISSISSIPPI IN SOUTHERN ILLINOIS. TOGETHER, THESE THREE GREAT RIVERS AND THEIR TRIBUTARIES PROVIDE IRRIGATION TO THE ENTIRE AGRICULTURAL REGION BETWEEN THE APPALACHIAN AND ROCKY MOUNTAINS – IN THE VAST MIDWESTERN AREA KNOWN AS THE "BREADBASKET OF AMERICA."

FARTHER TO THE WEST, THE COLORADO RIVER CARVES A MUCH MORE DRAMATIC, TURBULENT PATH THAN ITS EASTERN COUSINS. THE COLORADO ORIGINATES IN THE ROCKY MOUNTAINS, AND THEN TUMBLES AND CRASHES NEARLY 9,000 FEET (2,743 M) ALONG ITS 1,450-MILE (2,334-KM) JOURNEY TO THE

INTRODUCTION Majestic Waterways

GULF OF CALIFORNIA IN MEXICO. THE RIVER'S MOST SPECTACU-
LAR SECTION IS AT THE BOTTOM OF THE GRAND CANYON IN ARI-
ZONA, WHERE THE RIVER CONTINUES TO CARVE ITS IMPRESSIVE
PATH THROUGH THE ANCIENT ROCKS, AS IT HAS FOR AT LEAST
17 MILLION YEARS.

IN THE PACIFIC NORTHWEST, THE COLUMBIA RIVER RISES
FROM THE CANADIAN ROCKIES TO FLOW 1,243 MILES (2,000 KM)
THROUGH WASHINGTON AND OREGON BEFORE EMPTYING INTO
THE PACIFIC OCEAN. THE COLUMBIA'S LARGEST TRIBUTARY, THE
SNAKE RIVER, SPRINGS FROM FAR BENEATH YELLOWSTONE NA-
TIONAL PARK IN WYOMING, AND WENDS ITS WAY 1,040 MILES
(1,674 KM) THROUGH THE FLAT, WIDE SNAKE RIVER PLAIN TO
JOIN THE COLUMBIA IN WESTERN WASHINGTON.

ALSO IN THE PACIFIC NORTHWEST LIES THE DEEPEST LAKE IN

INTRODUCTION Majestic Waterways

THE U.S.A., AND THE THIRD DEEPEST IN THE WORLD. CRATER LAKE, FORMED BY THE COLLAPSE OF MOUNT MAZAMA NEARLY 8,000 YEARS AGO, IS 1,949 FEET (594 M) AT ITS DEEPEST POINT. FARTHER SOUTH AND EAST IS LAKE TAHOE, THE POPULAR RECREATION AREA ON THE CALIFORNIA/NEVADA BORDER AND THE SECOND DEEPEST U.S. LAKE AT 1,645 FEET (501 M).

PERHAPS THE MOST UNIQUE BODY OF WATER IN THE U.S.A. IS GREAT SALT LAKE, THE LARGEST SALT LAKE IN THE WESTERN HEMISPHERE. AT A MAXIMUM DEPTH OF JUST 33 FEET (10 M), THIS EXTREMELY SHALLOW LAKE IS ALL THAT REMAINS OF A MUCH LARGER, PREHISTORIC SALT LAKE. GREAT SALT LAKE SUP-PORTS VERY LITTLE AQUATIC LIFE, BUT IT IS A CRUCIAL STOPOVER FOR MILLIONS OF MIGRATING BIRDS EACH YEAR.

THE LARGEST LAKE SYSTEM IN THE WORLD, AND HOME TO 20

Majestic Waterways
Introduction

PERCENT OF THE PLANET'S SURFACE FRESH WATER, IS THE GREAT LAKES OF THE NORTH CENTRAL UNITED STATES. LAKES HURON, MICHIGAN, ERIE, ONTARIO (THE SMALLEST) AND SUPERIOR (THE LARGEST AND DEEPEST) HAVE FOR CENTURIES SUPPORTED INDUSTRY AND COMMERCE, AND CURRENTLY PROVIDE DRINKING WATER FOR MORE THAN 22 MILLION PEOPLE. LAKES ERIE AND ONTARIO ARE CONNECTED BY THE NIAGARA RIVER, WHICH CRASHES SPECTACULARLY OVER NIAGARA FALLS, THE ICONIC TOURIST SPOT ON THE U.S./CANADIAN BORDER.

TOGETHER, THESE LAKES AND RIVERS AND THEIR LESSER-KNOWN SISTERS HAVE IN MANY WAYS CONTRIBUTED TO THE STORY OF AMERICA. WHETHER EXPLOITED OR PROTECTED BY HUMANS, THEY FLOW ON, TIMELESS AND AGELESS.

- One of nearly 50 waterfalls within the dramatic landscape that is Yellowstone National Park, Wyoming.

378-379 and 379 • Waterfalls crisscross nearly all of the Hawaiian Islands' tropical volcanic terrain. Left, Kalaupapa National Park on Molakai Island; right, Waimea Canyon, the "Grand Canyon of the Pacific," Kauai.

380-381 • Dogsledding across the frozen North Fork of the Koyukuk River, Alaska.

382-383 ● A river valley at Gates of the Arctic National Park, in Alaska.

383 ● A moose calf nursing at the Cheena River, in Alaska.

384-385 and 385 • Sockeye salmon swimming upriver to spawn, photographed at Katmai National Park and Preserve, Alaska.

386-387 • A grizzly bear cooling off in Halo Bay, part of the Katmai National Park and Preserve, Alaska.

Because of its high mountain locale and lack of tributaries, Crater Lake (Oregon) contains some of the world's least contaminated water.

390 ● At 620 feet (189 m), Multnomah Falls is the tallest waterfall in Oregon.

390-391 ● The twin waterfalls of Upper McCord Creek in the Columbia River Gorge National Scenic Area, Oregon.

- The largest river in the Pacific Northwest, the Columbia River forms much of the border between Washington and Oregon.

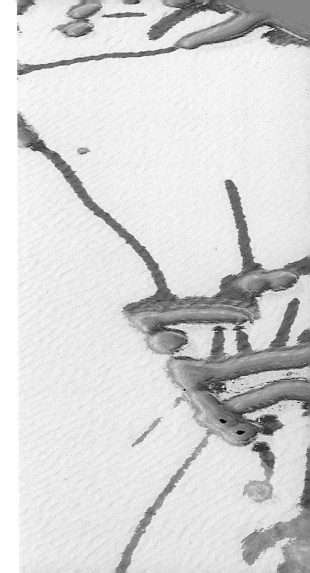

- Aerial views of the winterscape at Sequoia and Kings Canyon National Park, California.

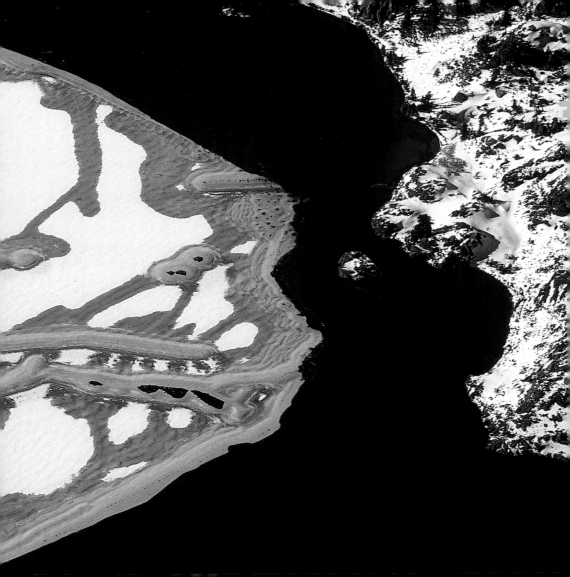

396 ● Fannette Island, Lake Tahoe's only island, located in Emerald Bay.

396-397 ● The aptly named Emerald Bay in winter, Lake Tahoe, California.

● Lake Skinner, a manmade reservoir in southern California, provides a picturesque setting for the annual Temecula Valley Balloon & Wine Festival.

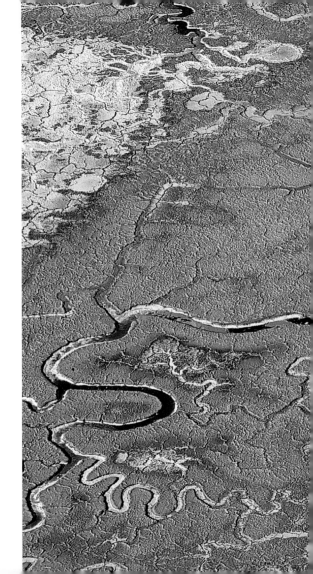

● The San Francisco Bay mudflats, top and right, are a key stopover on the Pacific Flyway, the annual flight path of millions of migrating birds.

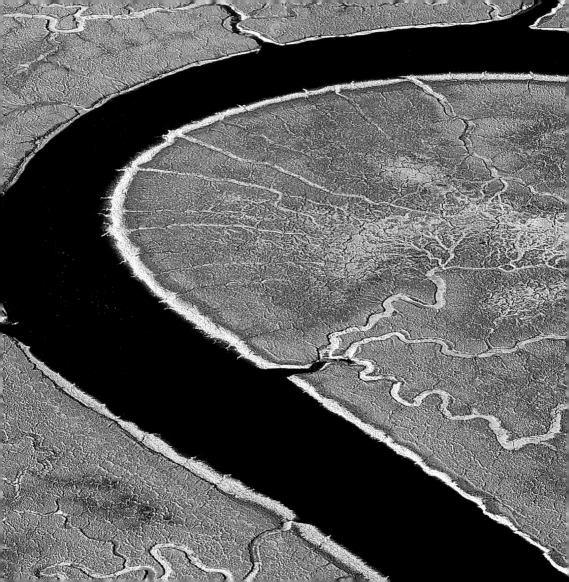

The hypersalinity and high alkaline content of Mono Lake (top) in eastern California support a type of brine shrimp found nowhere else, and formed these unique "Tufa Towers" (right).

404-405 ● Lake Mead, and the Lake Mead National Recreation Area, were formed by the 1936 completion of Hoover Dam across the Colorado River. The lake is now the largest reservoir in the U.S.A.

406-407 ● A network of lakes, ponds, rivers and streams enlaces Rocky Mountain National Park, Colorado.

Construction of the Glen Canyon Dam, a major source of hydroelectric power in Arizona and Utah, formed Lake Powell (right) and the Glen Canyon National Recreation Area.

As stunning as it is, Lake Powell, formed by the damming of the Colorado River, has been controversial from the start because it radically altered the natural flow of the Colorado River.

412 • A bridge over the Colorado River at Glen Canyon Recreation Area, Utah.

413 • The Colorado River flows through Marble Canyon in Arizona, near the Utah border.

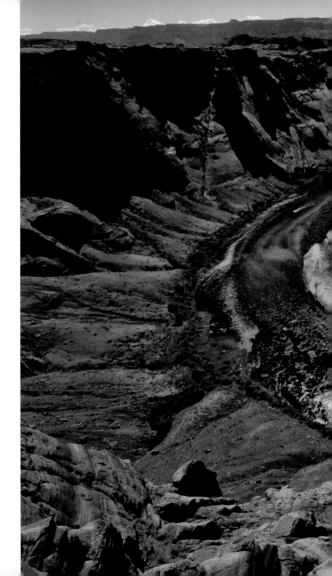

There's no mystery as to how Horseshoe Bend, on the Colorado River within Glen Canyon Recreation Area, Arizona, got its name.

A lake on the Arizona-New Mexico border and within the Navajo Nation, a semi-autonomous region of Native Americans that includes parts of Utah as well.

Sandhill Cranes (top) and Snow Geese (right) winter by the tens of thousands at Bosque Del Apache National Wildlife Reserve, New Mexico.

420 • The confluence of the
Yellowstone River with the
Missouri River – the U.S.A.'s
longest – in North Dakota.

420-421 • The White Cliffs tower
over the Upper Missouri as it flows
through Montana.

● Steam rises from one of
Yellowstone National Park's
(Wyoming) 10,000 geothermal
areas, the best-known of which is
the Old Faithful Geyser, right.

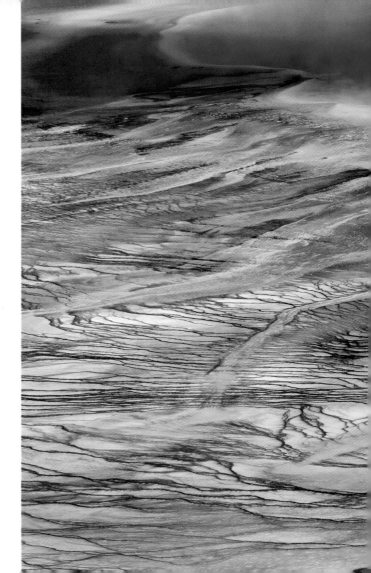

The Midway Geyser Basin at Yellowstone National Park, Wyoming. Rudyard Kipling dubbed the range of boiling geothermal waters "Hell's Half Acre."

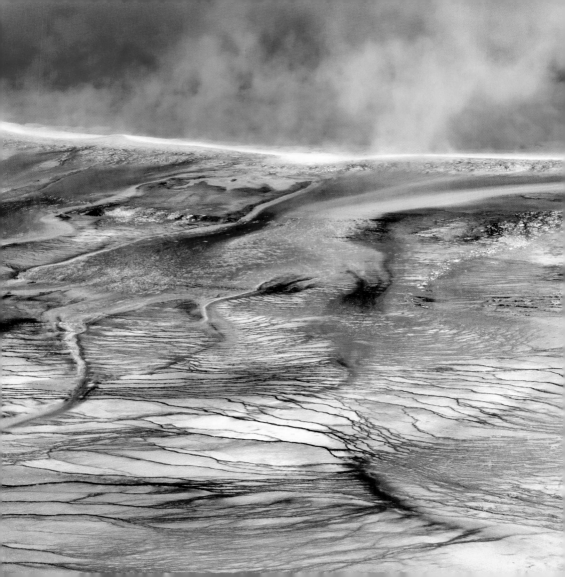

426 ● A moose wades through the Snake River at Grand Teton National Park, Wyoming.

426-427 ● The Yellowstone River meanders through a valley in Yellowstone National Park, Wyoming.

● The mighty Mississippi River near New Orleans, and the Mississippi Delta as it nears the Gulf of Mexico in Louisiana.

430 • A prehistoric predator, this algae-covered alligator lolls in a Louisiana bayou.

430-431 • Cypress trees in fall foliage rise from duckweed-blanketed Heron Pond in the Cache River wetlands in southern Illinois, the northernmost site of cypress trees in the U.S.A.

432-433 ● One of the many bends in the Mississippi River as it flows through Tennessee.

433 ● The John F. Kennedy Memorial Bridge crosses the Ohio River and connects Louisville, Kentucky to Jeffersonville, Indiana.

434 ● The Pointe Aux Barques Lighthouse on Lake Huron, near Port Hope, Michigan.

435 ● Waves ripple ashore at Miner's Beach on Lake Superior, Pictured Rocks National Lakeshore, Michigan.

Largely icebound in winter, Lake Michigan is the second largest of the five Great Lakes and is bounded by Wisconsin, Michigan, Illinois and Indiana.

438-439 ● Icejams like this on Lake Michigan are common and costly: they often block shipping routes between the Great Lakes and can cause flooding when the ice finally breaks up.

440-441 ● Some of the many lighthouses lining the shores of Lake Michigan. Most were built in the late 1800s to safely guide ships traversing the Great Lakes.

● Niagara Falls forms the dramatic border between New York and Ontario, Canada. Top: The American Falls of Niagara; right: larger Horseshoe Falls, two-thirds of which lies in Canada.

444-445 ● A winter scene at Niagara Falls.

445 ● Tibbetts Point Lighthouse on Lake Ontario, New York.

446-447 ● One of New Hampshire's countless woodland waterfalls, Arethusa Falls creates an ethereal mist in the White Mountains.

447 ● The Pondicherry Wildlife Refuge in New Hampshire's White Mountains is an important bird habitat – more than 200 species have been recorded here.

448-449 and 449 ● The "River of Grass," the slow-moving freshwater body that forms Everglades National Park, empties into the Florida Bay. Long ago altered by human intervention, it is now undergoing a major restoration.

450-451 ● Rare White Pelicans rest under a setting sun in the shallow waters of Everglades National Park, Florida.

TOWERING SENTINELS

- Fiery fall colors are reflected in a lake in the White Mountains of New Hampshire.

INTRODUCTION Towering Sentinels

IN THE UNITED STATES AND IN THE REST OF THE WORLD, PERHAPS NO ECOSYSTEMS HAVE SUFFERED SO MUCH AT THE HANDS OF HUMANS AS HAVE THE FORESTS. LONG EXPLOITED FOR TIMBER AND TO MAKE WAY FOR DEVELOPMENT, FORESTS OF THE U.S.A. HAVE FALLEN AT AN ALARMING RATE, PARTICULARLY IN THE 19TH AND 20TH CENTURIES BEFORE THE ERA OF RESPONSIBLE FOREST STEWARDSHIP. TODAY AMERICA'S REMAINING OLD GROWTH FORESTS STAND AS DEFIANT ANCIENT TEMPLES, AND SEEM TO SIT IN SILENT JUDGMENT OF HOW WELL WE CHOOSE TO PROTECT THEM.

A FOREST IS CONSIDERED "OLD-GROWTH" OR PRIMEVAL WHEN IT CONTAINS STANDS OF VERY OLD TREES AND HAS WITNESSED A MINIMAL AMOUNT OF HUMAN ACTIVITY AND DISTURBANCE. WHEN GIANT TREES FALL NATURALLY, LIGHT PENE-

INTRODUCTION Towering Sentinels

TRATES THE CANOPY AND SPURS GROWTH ON THE FOREST FLOOR. FROM THE ROTTING LOGS ON THE FOREST FLOOR TO THE HIGHEST REACHES OF THE VERDANT CANOPY, THESE ELEMENTS COMBINE TO FORM UNIQUE ECOSYSTEMS THAT SHELTER MANY RARE AND ENDANGERED SPECIES OF PLANTS AND ANIMALS. THIRTY-FOUR STATES IN THE U.S.A. CONTAIN AT LEAST SOME OLD-GROWTH FOREST, THOUGH THEIR AREAS RANGE FROM VERY SMALL – JUST 5 ACRES [2 HA]) ON BEAR MOUNTAIN IN CONNECTICUT – TO IMMENSE – THE 5 MILLION ACRES (2 MILLION HA) TONGASS NATIONAL FOREST IN ALASKA.

THE BEST KNOWN OLD-GROWTH FORESTS IN AMERICA – THOSE IN CALIFORNIA – OFFER MANY SUPERLATIVES: HYPERION IN REDWOODS NATIONAL PARK, A COASTAL REDWOOD THAT MEASURES 379 FEET [115.6 M], IS THE TALLEST TREE IN THE

WORLD, THOUGH A MERE 600 YEARS OLD. THE OLDEST TREE IN THE U.S.A. – AND UNTIL RECENTLY CONSIDERED THE OLDEST IN THE WORLD – IS METHUSELAH, A BRISTLECONE PINE FOUND IN THE INYO NATIONAL FOREST. AT NEARLY 4,800 YEARS OLD, METHUSELAH IS AS OLD AS THE GREAT PYRAMIDS OF GIZA, EGYPT, AND MILLENNIA OLDER THAN THE ROMAN EMPIRE, STONEHENGE, AND THE GREAT WALL OF CHINA. GENERAL SHERMAN IS A GIANT SEQUOIA IN CALIFORNIA'S SEQUOIA NA-TIONAL PARK: THOUGH NOT AS TALL (275 FEET, OR 84 M) AS HIS COASTAL CALIFORNIA COUSINS, GENERAL SHERMAN IS THE WORLD'S LARGEST TREE – HIS GIRTH IS A STAGGERING 103 FEET, OR MORE THAN 31 METERS.

BUT BEYOND THESE IMPRESSIVE STATISTICS, THESE AN-CIENT FORESTS – AND THE EQUALLY IMPRESSIVE FORESTS OF

INTRODUCTION Towering Sentinels

OREGON, WYOMING, MONTANA, IDAHO, COLORADO AND MANY OTHER WESTERN STATES – OFFER THE RARE OPPORTUNITY TO COMMUNE IN SOLITUDE WITH UNPOLLUTED NATURE, AND THE HUMBLING EXPERIENCE OF BEING A SMALL CREATURE AMIDST THESE TOWERING GREEN GIANTS.

THOUGH THE MAJORITY OF REMAINING LARGE FOREST TRACTS LIE WEST OF THE MISSISSIPPI RIVER, NEW ENGLAND AND THE EASTERN SEABOARD ALSO BOAST IMPRESSIVE FORESTS, SUCH AS THOSE OF THE SCENIC WHITE MOUNTAINS OF NEW HAMPSHIRE AND THE GREEN MOUNTAINS OF VERMONT, WHERE MAPLE, BEECH AND BIRCH TREES DAZZLE WITH THEIR VIBRANT, COLORFUL PALETTE OF CHANGING AUTUMN LEAVES.

THE FORESTS OF TENNESSEE AND NORTH CAROLINA ARE HOME TO COUNTLESS VARIETIES OF SONGBIRDS, DEER AND

Towering Sentinels

Introduction

BLACK BEARS. FARTHER SOUTH, CYPRESS FORESTS IN MISSIS-SIPPI, ALABAMA, GEORGIA AND FLORIDA PROVIDE SWAMPY REFUGE FOR ALLIGATORS, TURTLES, FISH AND WADING BIRDS, INCLUDING RARE AND ENDANGERED SPECIES OF WOOD STORK, PELICANS AND WOODPECKERS.

AMERICA'S FORESTS SERVE AS THE LUNGS OF OUR LAND-SCAPE, AND THE BAROMETERS OF THE ENVIRONMENTAL HEALTH OF THE COUNTRY. BUT EVEN MORE THAN THAT, THEY ARE THE TOWERING GREEN SENTINELS THAT INVITE US TO RE-MEMBER THAT WE ARE BUT TEMPORARY GUESTS AMONG THEIR TRUNKS AND BRANCHES, AND THAT THEIR TIMELESS PERSEVERANCE, LIKE THAT OF NATURE HERSELF, CONTINUES WITH OR WITHOUT US.

- Aerial view of forest and meadows in Yellowstone National Park, Wyoming, the world's first national park.

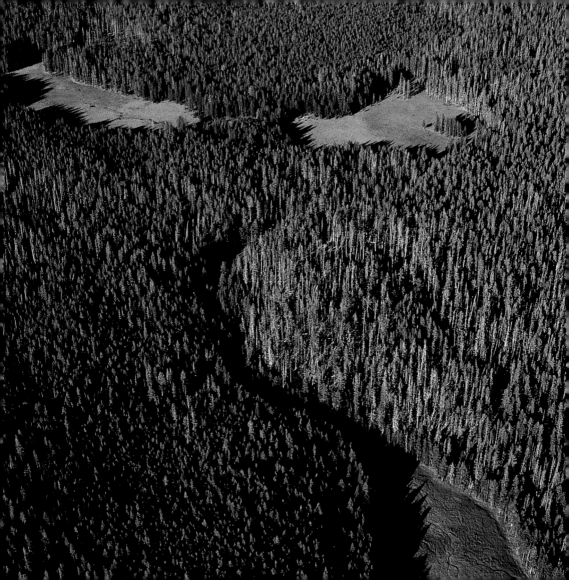

460 ● A wolf hunts in Denali National Park and Preserve, Alaska.

460-461 ● Autumn tundra creates a colorful carpet in one of Denali's relatively flat areas.

462 and 462-463 • Giant Sequoia (bottom) and Coastal Redwoods (right) are some of the world's largest trees; both are found in California.

464-465 • White Mountains National Park in California is home to one of the world's oldest trees, an ancient bristlecone pine named Methuselah.

Two superstars of the Montana glacial forest and meadows, a bison with young (top), and a grizzly bear on the prowl (right).

468-469 and 469 • Evergreen Douglas Fir stand side by side with deciduous aspen, spruce and cottonwood trees in Gallatin National Forest, Montana.

470-471 • Towering mountains form the backdrop of a wintry landscape in Grand Teton National Park, Wyoming.

472-473 • Grey wolves, like this trio in Idaho, are pack animals with extremely complex social hierarchies.

474 and 474-475 ● Winter snowfall in Yellowstone National Park means that animals have to work harder to find food. Here, elk (bottom) and bison (right) forage in the snowy landscape.

476-477 ● Summertime forest in Yellowstone National Park, Wyoming, where large predators include grey wolves, grizzly bears and mountain lions.

478-479 • An evergreen forest in Rocky Mountain National Park near Silverton, Colorado.

480-481 • Moose, like this one at Sprague Lake in Rocky Mountain National Park, were introduced to Colorado in the 1970s.

● A forested slope at Maroon Bells, near Aspen, Colorado, reputedly one of the most photographed spots in the state.

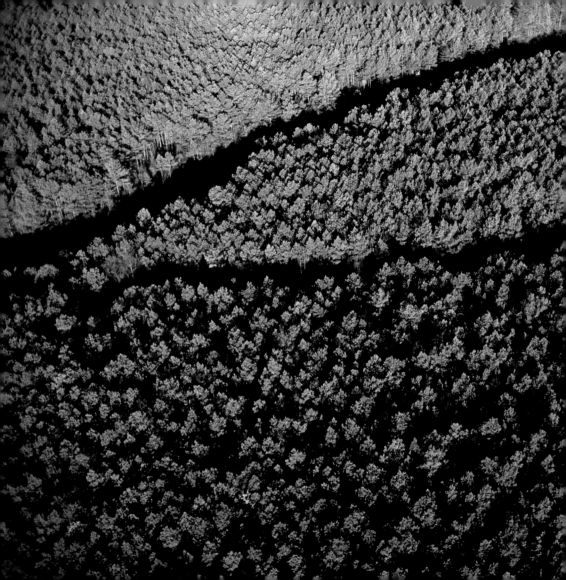

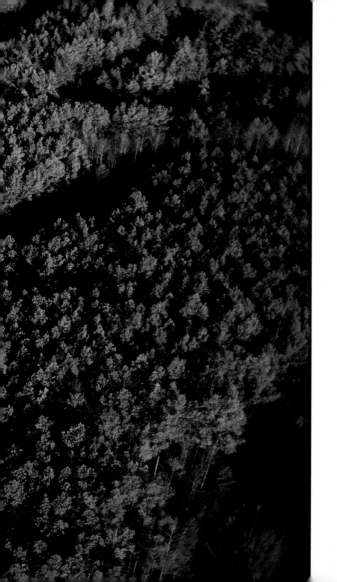

Pine forest in the Cumberland Plateau, Tennessee, a region crisscrossed by rivers and streams, and resplendent with waterfalls.

● Bald cypress trees in the morning mist at Spring Lake, Wall Doxey State Park, Mississippi, left, and above, at Merchants Millpond State Park, North Carolina.

The first flashes of autumn color arrive in the White Mountains of New Hampshire, seen here at a riverbank near North Woodstock (left) and at Bear Notch (top).

The Green Mountains of Vermont hardly live up to their name in winter; here they are seen cloaked in a heavy blanket of snow.

Maple, birch, poplar and hickory trees vie for attention during their annual autumn displays of color, seen here in the White Mountains of New Hampshire.

● Brilliant fall foliage shimmers in the mist-shrouded waters of Molly's Falls Pond near Marshfield, Vermont.

INDEX

INDEX

INDEX

PHOTOGRAPHIC CREDITS

PHOTOGRAPHIC CREDITS

page 219 Massimo Borchi/Archivio White Star
pages 220-221, 221 Antonio Attini/Archivio White Star
pages 222-223 Greg Pease/Getty Images
page 224 Antonio Attini/Archivio White Star
pages 224-225 Andrew Gunner/Getty Images
pages 226-227 Mitchell Funk/Getty Images
pages 228-229 Antonio Attini/Archivio White Star
page 230 Mitchell Funk/Getty Images
page 230-231 Mitchell Funk/Getty Images
pages 232-233, 234, 235 Antonio Attini/Archivio White Star
pages 236-237 Ellen Rooney/Getty Images
pages 238-239 Travelpix Ltd/Getty Images
pages 240-241, 242-243 Massimo Borchi/Archivio White Star
page 245 Inga Spence/Getty Images
pages 251 Martin Ruegner/Getty Images
pages 252-253 Antonio Attini/Archivio White Star
pages 254-255 Willard Clay/Getty Images
pages 256-257 Sunset Avenue Productions/Getty Images
pages 258-259 Bob Pool/Getty Images
pages 260, 260-261 Antonio Attini/Archivio White Star
pages 262-263 Glowimages/Getty Images
page 264 Andy Sacks/Getty Images
page 265 Ed Darack/Getty Images
pages 266-267, 267 Antonio Attini/Archivio White Star
page 268 Karen Kasmauski/Getty Images
pages 268-269 Medioimages/Photodisc/Getty Images
pages 270-271 Chris Leschinsky/Getty Images
pages 272-273 Thomas Jackson/Getty Images
page 274 Cameron Davidson/Getty Images
pages 274-275 Cameron Davidson/Getty Images
pages 276-277 Panoramic Images/Getty Images
pages 278-279 Massimo Borchi/Archivio White Star
pages 280-281 Andy Sacks/Getty Images
pages 282-283 Harrison Shull/Getty Images
pages 284-285 Massimo Borchi/Archivio White Star
pages 286-287 Altrendo Nature/Getty Images
pages 288-289, 289 Massimo Borchi/Archivio White Star
pages 290-291 Pete TurnerGetty Images
pages 292-293 V. Gianella/De Agostini Picture Library
page 294 Martin Ruegner/Getty Images:
pages 294-295 Cameron Davidson/Getty Images
page 296 Harrison Shull/Getty Images
pages 296-297 Harald Sund/Getty Images
pages 298-299 Barrie Rokeach/Getty Images
page 301 Antonio Attini/Archivio White Star
page 307 Marcello Bertinetti/Archivio White Star
pages 308-309 Marc Adamus/Getty Images
pages 310-311 Jeff Hunter/Getty Images
pages 312-313 Bill Wight CA/ Getty Images
pages 314-315, 316-317 Marcello Bertinetti/Archivio White Star
pages 318-319 Panoramic Images/Getty Images
pages 320-321 Carr Clifton/Getty Images
pages 322, 322-323, 324-325, 326-327, 328-329, 330, 330-331 Antonio Attini/Archivio White Star
pages 332-333 David Costa/Getty Images
pages 334-335, 336-337, 338, 338-339, 340-341, 342-343, 344, 345, 346, 347, 348-349, 349, 350 Antonio Attini/Archivio White Star
page 351 Carr Clifton/Getty Images
pages 352-353 Massimo Borchi/Archivio White Star
pages 354-355 Ryan McVay/Getty Images
pages 356-357 L. Romano/De Agostini Picture Library
pages 358-359 Ed Darack/Getty Images
pages 360-361 G. Cozzi/De Agostini Picture Library
pages 362-363, 364, 364-365, 366-367 Massimo Borchi/Archivio White Star
pages 368-369 Antonio Attini/Archivio White Star
page 371 Stephen Alvarez/Getty Images
pages 377, 378-379, 379 Antonio Attini/Archivio White Star
pages 380-381 David Madison/Getty Images
pages 382-383 M. Santini/De Agostini Picture Library:
pages 383 Michael S. Quinton/Getty Images
pages 384-385 Michael Melford/Getty Images
pages 385 Werner Van Steen/Getty Images
pages 386-387 Matthew Scholey/Getty Images
pages 388-389 Alan Kearney/Getty Images
pages 390 Robert Glusic/Getty Images
pages 390-391 Danielle D. Hughson/Getty Images
pages 392-393 Larry Gloth/Getty Images
pages 394, 394-395 Antonio Attini/Archivio White Star
page 396 Dennis Flaherty//Getty Images
pages 396-397 Thinkstock/Getty Images
pages 398-399 Michael J. Slezak/Getty Images
pages 400, 400-401 Antonio Attini/Archivio White Star
page 402 Don Smith/Getty Images
pages 402-403 Don Smith/Getty Images
pages 404-405 Ian Shive/Getty Images
pages 406-407 Massimo Borchi/Archivio White Star
pages 408, 408-409, 410, 411 Antonio Attini/Archivio White Star
page 412 David Schultz//Getty Images

Cover, from left

first rank: Antonio Attini/Archivio White Star, Antonio Attini/Archivio White Star , Marcello Bertinetti/Archivio White Star

second rank: Antonio Attini/Archivio White Star, Antonio Attini/Archivio White Star, Antonio Attini/Archivio White Star

third rank: Antonio Attini/Archivio White Star , Antonio Attini/Archivio White Star , Marcello Bertinetti/Archivio White Star

Back cover, from left

first rank: Antonio Attini/Archivio White Star, Massimo Borchi/Archivio White Star, Antonio Attini/Archivio White Star

second rank: Massimo Borchi/Archivio White Star, Massimo Borchi/Archivio White Star, Antonio Attini/Archivio White Star

third rank: Antonio Attini/Archivio White Star, Antonio Attini/Archivio White Star, Massimo Borchi/Archivio White Star

Elizabeth Heath is an American-born freelance writer and editor now living in central Italy. She was born in St. Louis, Missouri, was raised in Florida and lived for several years in Washington, DC. She has written art, entertainment, interior design, outdoors, lifestyle and travel articles for national and regional magazines, newspapers and websites.
Heath has degrees in Fine Arts and Humanities, and is currently completing her Ph.D. in anthropology and archaeology at USF, with a focus on the presentation of public archaeology in Italy.

Cover ● From left:
first rank - Mount Rushmore National Memorial (South Dakota); Empire State Building (New York City); Alaska Range.
second rank - Monument Valley (Utah/Arizona); Big Sur (California); Golden Gate Bridge (San Francisco).
third rank - Bryce Canyon National Park (Utah); Yellowstone National Park (Wyoming); Key Biscayne (Miami, Florida).

● One of the twin "Mittens" of Monument Valley, Arizona.

Back cover ● From left:
first rank - Grand Canyon National Park (Arizona); US Capitol (Washington DC); Arches National Park (Utah).
second rank - Addison County (Vermont); Taos Pueblo (New Mexico); Chicago (Illinois).
third rank - Tower Fall (Yellowstone National Park, Wyoming); Yellowstone National Park (Wyoming); Mohawk Trail State Forest (Massachusetts).